TOP 50

All New!

Instant

Bible Lessons®

for Elementary

ROSEKiDZ®

Top 50 Instant Bible Lessons® for Elementary

©2016 by Rose Publishing, LLC

Published by RoseKidz®
A division of Tyndale House Ministries
Rose Publishing, LLC
P.O. Box 3473
Peabody, Massachusetts 01961-3473 USA
www.hendricksonpublishinggroup.com

Writer: Lindsey Whitney
Cover Illustrator: Chad Thompson
Interior Designer: Terrill Thomas

Unless otherwise noted, Scripture is taken from the Holy Bible, New International Version®, NIV®. Copyright© 1973, 1978, 1984, 2011 by Biblica, Inc.™ Used by permission of Zondervan. All rights reserved worldwide. www.zondervan.com The "NIV" and "New International Version" and are trademarks registered in the United States Patent and Trademark Office by Biblica, Inc.™

ISBN: 978-1-62862-498-4
R50003
RELIGION/Christian Ministry/Children

Printed in the United States of America
Printed September 2021

Contents

Contents, continued

INTRODUCTION

Top 50 Instant Bible Lessons for Elementary

What are the most important Bible lessons each child should know? There are many to choose from, but we have assembled what can easily be argued as fifty of the top Bible stories for children. In this volunteer-friendly book, you will find all you need to connect the heart and mind of each child to God's Word and truth.

It is well known that if you just lecture teach a child they will inevitably check out after a few minutes and miss all the valuable information you are trying to share. Each of these lessons is designed to reinforce the BIG IDEA Bible truth each step of the way. All the while, the children will be engaged and interacting with you and the story. Each lesson includes a Bible Story, Object Lesson, Opening Game and Additional Optional Activities.

Each lesson comes with a quick reference materials list and step-by-step instructions on what to do and say all along the way. Throughout the book you will find tips, "Tidbits" on Development, Behavior Management, Learning Styles and Volunteers. Use these tidbits for workshops or on social media to encourage and educate those in this most important mission field.

How To Use This Book

Each chapter begins with the focus Scripture and memory verse. The Big Idea helps you keep children focused on the main truth being taught from God's Word. Be sure to draw attention to it and emphasize it all throughout the lesson. The Overview will give you some history and prepare you for teaching the lesson. The Bible Story opens God's Word and begins the learning.

Children will love the Opening Game and Object Lesson. Wrap up the lesson by choosing any or all of the Additional Optional Activities. These activities allow children with different learning styles to get more time with the Bible truth. And they allow you to tailor the lesson to the time you have in your schedule.

Most lessons come with reproducible pages in the back of the book.

Chapter I: Creation

BIBLE STORY REFERENCE: Genesis 1:1–31

MEMORY VERSE: *In the beginning God created the heavens and the earth. Genesis 1:1*

Big Idea
God Made All Things

Overview

Say: God is so powerful that he made the entire world, simply by speaking. God made the light, the water, the plants, the animals, and even people! Because God is so powerful and strong, we can trust him. Today, we will learn that **God made all things**. *(Open with prayer requests, praises, and a time of prayer.)*

Bible Story

Say: Where is the darkest place you have ever been? *(Children respond.)* In today's Bible story, God creates the entire world out of nothing! Before God began creating things, everything was dark and formless. Let's read the Bible at Genesis 1:1–5. *(Read Scripture aloud.)* That is pretty amazing! Not only did God create light, he also made the sun, moon, and stars to give us light all the time. Let's read Genesis 1:14–19. *(Read Scripture aloud.)* God also made the plants, trees, animals, rivers, lakes, birds, fish, and everything you see in nature. God created humans to rule over the things on the earth. *(Read Genesis 1:26–27.)* God was very happy with the things that he made. *(Read Genesis 1:31.)* It would have been amazing to see all those things at the beginning of Creation. I am so glad that **God made all things**.

Outline
Overview
Bible Story
Opening Game
Object Lesson
Additional Optional Activities

Materials
- Bibles
- Reproducible page 210
- Yellow or white construction paper
- Orange
- Knife
- Olive oil
- Lighter or matches
- Plastic knives
- Yellow frosting
- Cupcakes
- Candy corn
- Variety of lighting
- Blanket or sheet
- Chairs

Opening Game: Hidden Stars

Materials
- Yellow or white construction paper

Added Bonus: Place one word from the memory verse on each star. Challenge the children to work together to make as many intact verses as possible.

Alternate Idea: To make the game more challenging for older kids, make different colors of stars. Have a scoring system for the different colors of stars.

Preparation: Copy and cut stars from construction paper using the template below. Hide the stars throughout the room.

Say: In today's Bible story we read in Genesis 1:14–19 that God spoke and everything in nature appeared. Today, we're going to pretend that the stars are missing and you have to find them! You'll have two minutes to find as many stars as possible.

Directions: Children search throughout the room to find the missing stars. After two minutes, gather children and have them count their stars. The child with the most stars tells something God made. If time permits, have one or two kids hide the stars in the room and play game again.

Materials

- Orange
- Knife
- Olive oil
- Lighter or matches

Tip: For a great visual tutorial on how to make the orange candle, search online by typing "How to make a candle out of an orange video."

Say: Today we're going to make our own sun out of an orange. Does anyone know why the sun is so bright? (*Children respond.*) **The real sun burns gas to stay bright, but our little orange sun is going to burn oil.**

Directions: Using the knife, score the orange peel around the middle of the orange, cutting just the peel and not into the fruit. Carefully, separate the rind away from the fruit, producing two small cups from the orange peel. Set the fruit aside for later.

At the bottom of the orange, there will be a small membrane (the central core) inside the orange. Peel the rind away in a way that leaves this small membrane attached to the bottom half of the rind. This will serve as your wick.

Pour oil onto the wick and into the bottom half of the now hollowed out orange. As you wait for the wick to soak up the oil a bit, cut a small hole in the top half of the rind to allow air into the orange candle. Light the wick and replace the now hollow top to create a small orange sun. Place it in a dark place to really see it glow.

Say: This is a just a small version of our amazing sun, but it's still pretty cool. It is so amazing that **God made all things**, including the sun, stars, and moon. And this is just the beginning! I can't wait to hear more from God's Word!

Additional Optional Activities

Materials
- Plastic knives
- Yellow frosting
- Cupcakes
- Candy corn

Sunshine Cupcake

Say: God made all things, including the sun, moon, and stars. Let's do a little creating of our own.

Directions: Children use knives to frost cupcakes. Place the candy corn around the edge of the cupcake with the points facing out to look like the rays of the sun. Eat and enjoy!

Materials
- Variety of lighting (Flashlights, glow sticks, battery-operated tea lights, glow in the dark stars, battery-operated lanterns, etc.)
- Blanket or sheet

Shine a Light

Preparation: Place a blanket or sheet over a table, dropping the cloth down one or more sides to create a dark space under the table.

Say: God made lights so that we can see both in the day and night. Did you know that the Bible also tells us that Jesus is the light of the world? (*Read John 8:12.*) **Even a little light can make a big difference in a dark place. Jesus is the light of the world, and he calls us to be light to others as well. Let's talk about ways we can share the light of Jesus with others.**

Directions: Children pick a type of light to use in the dark space you prepared.

Materials
- Reproducible page 210
- Chairs

Upset the Solar System

Preparation: Copy and cut out cards on page 210, making two or more copies so that there is at least one card for each child.

Say: God made all things, including all the planets. Today we are going to play a fun game and mix up all the planets.

Directions: Hand one card to each child in the group. It is good if multiple kids have the same planet. Players sit in chairs in a circle, with one child in the middle (without a chair). The middle child calls out a planet and whoever has that planet must get up and find a new chair. Meanwhile, the child in the middle tries to steal a chair. Whoever is left without a chair calls the new planet. Kids may call multiple planets at once or they may say "Upset the Solar System" and everyone has to get up and move.

Chapter 2: Sin Enters the World

BIBLE STORY REFERENCE: Genesis 2:8—3:23

MEMORY VERSE: *The Lord God commanded the man, "You are free to eat from any tree in the garden; but you must not eat from the tree of the knowledge of good and evil, for when you eat from it you will certainly die." Genesis 2:16–17*

Big Idea
Sin Destroys the Good Things God Makes

Overview

Say: God made an amazing world filled with all kinds of things. When the world first began, everything was perfect. Adam and Eve, the first people, lived in a beautiful place called the Garden of Eden. However, Adam and Eve chose to disobey God and they lost the perfect world they lived in. Today, we will learn that **sin destroys the good things God makes.** (*Open with prayer requests, praises, and a time of prayer.*)

Bible Story

Say: In today's Bible story, Adam and Eve lived in a perfect place. It was happy and safe. The best part about living in the Garden of Eden was the chance to be with God. Let's turn in the Bible to Genesis 2:8–9.

If you could hang out with God for a day, what kinds of things would you like to do? (*Children respond.*)

Those things sound like a lot of fun. Maybe Adam and Eve did some of those things, too. Unfortunately, Adam and Eve made a bad choice and disobeyed God. Because they sinned, their perfect place was destroyed. Let's keep reading. (*Read Genesis 3:1–7 and Genesis 3:23.*) What a sad day for Adam and Eve. Remember, **sin destroys the good things God makes.**

Outline
Overview
Bible Story
Opening Game
Object Lesson
Additional Optional Activities

Materials
- **Bibles**
- **Reproducible page 211**
- **Bubble wand and solution**
- **Balloon**
- **Safety pin**
- **Permanent marker**
- **Red, green, and brown construction paper**
- **Glue**
- **Red pompoms**
- **Lunch-sized paper bags**

Opening Game: Don't Pop the Bubble

Materials

- Bubble wand and solution

Say: In today's Bible story, God gave Adam and Eve some specific instructions about a tree in the middle of the garden. They were not to eat from the tree of the knowledge of good and evil. Adam and Eve did not obey God's instructions. Sometimes it's easy to obey instructions and sometimes it is not. Sometimes we are tempted to disobey, just like Adam and Eve were. Today, we're going to practice following instructions, even when we are tempted.

Directions: Blow some bubbles. For a few minutes, kids pop the bubbles. Next, children sit on the floor. Blow some more bubbles, instructing children to not pop the bubbles. Some children will find it very hard to resist!

Play a few rounds, sometimes allowing kids to move around and pop the bubbles and sometimes instructing them to sit and not pop the bubbles.

DEVELOPMENTAL TIDBITS

What are school-aged children capable of learning about God?

- Discovering the transforming power of the Bible and how to use it.
- Starting to grasp abstract concepts—baptism, Communion, the Trinity
- Understanding the power of prayer and using it.
- Understand spiritual gifts
- Serving the world with their time and talents
- Learning to share their faith—reaching out to others intentionally
- Choosing healthy friendships and boundaries
- Developing a Christian worldview—critical viewing of media

See page 11 for more insights into school-aged children.

Object Lesson: Balloon Pop

Materials

- Balloon
- Safety pin
- Permanent marker

Prep: Blow up balloon in front of kids and tie it shut.

Say: Do you guys remember some of the cool stuff we mentioned before? Stuff we would want in a perfect world? Tell me what they are. (*Children respond. Write responses on the outside of the balloon.*)

Let's imagine that this balloon is our perfect world. It's got all our cool stuff written on it. Unfortunately, it's not going to stay this way for long. Take a look at this. (*Hold up the pin for the kids to see.*) Imagine that this pin is sin, or the bad choices that we make. What do you think will happen if sin enters our perfect world? (*Children respond.*)

I think you are right! Just like sin destroys the good things God makes, this pin would destroy our perfect world. (*Use the pin to pop the balloon.*)

Wow, that makes me feel pretty sad. How about you? Just like sin destroys the good things God makes, that pin destroyed our perfect world. And now, there is nothing we can do to make it whole again.

Just like Adam and Eve had to leave their perfect garden and never go back, we can't fix our broken world either. It was a very sad day for them, but God had a plan to fix their mistake, which we will hear more about later!

Materials

- Reproducible page 211
- Red and green construction paper

Red Light Green Light

Say: Adam and Eve should have stopped when God told them to. In this game, you will need to obey instructions just like Adam and Eve.

Preparation: Photocopy page 211 to create a red "Stop" sign and a green "Go" sign out of construction paper.

Directions: Line kids up across the room and have them advance towards you when you hold up the green sign and stop when you hold up the red sign. Anyone who disobeys the signs must go back to the starting line. The first child to reach you gets a turn to use the signs.

Materials

- Green and brown construction paper
- Glue
- Red pompoms

Bonus Idea: Children draw or cut out animal pictures to glue around the tree.

For Younger Kids: Prepare trunk and treetops before class.

Trees of Creation

Say: We don't really know what kind of fruit was on the tree of knowledge of good and evil, but we do know that there was fruit. In fact, there were lots of fruit trees in the Garden of Eden. Let's create some interesting looking trees together.

Directions: Children make a tree trunk out of brown construction paper and a tree top out of green construction paper. Glue pieces onto a piece of thick cardstock. Then, glue pompoms onto the tree to make 3-D art representing one of the trees in the Garden of Eden.

Materials

- Lunch-sized paper bags, one for each child

Tip: If you can't go outside, bring in a nature book. As you turn the pages, play "I Spy" using colors of the rainbow.

God Made All Things

Say: Last week, we learned that God made all things. Even though **sin destroys the good things God makes**, there is still plenty we can appreciate about Creation. Let's take a walk to see what we can find.

Directions: Take the kids outside for nature walk and talk about your favorite things that God made. See if you can find all the colors in the rainbow. Ask the kids about their favorite spot to go when they are outside or about their favorite animal. Collect items from nature to take home and share with their family about the amazing things God has made.

Chapter 3: Noah's Ark

BIBLE STORY REFERENCE: Genesis 6:5–19

MEMORY VERSE: *Noah did everything just as God commanded him. Genesis 6:22*

Big Idea
God Does Not Like Sin

Overview

Say: After Adam and Eve left the Garden of Eden, they had children. Those children had children and soon, the whole world was filled with people. Sadly, many of those people did not obey God. **God does not like sin** and it hurt his heart to see the bad choices the people were making. There was one man, however, that loved God and obeyed him. His name was Noah. (*Open with prayer requests, praises, and a time of prayer.*)

Bible Story

Say: Have you ever made a bad choice? Did anything happen because of your bad choice? Did something break or someone get hurt? (*Children respond.*)

In today's Bible story, the people of the world were making all kinds of bad choices. They were not listening to God and they were ruining the world that he had made. **God does not like sin** and he had to do something about all the people who were being disobedient. (*Read Genesis 6:5–8.*)

There was one man, named Noah, who loved God and obeyed what God said. God told Noah to build a giant boat called an ark. God was going to save Noah, Noah's family, and some of the animals in the world, but he was going to destroy everything else. Let's keep reading. (*Read Genesis 6:13–14 and Genesis 6:17–19.*)

God was very sad, but he could not let people continue to sin. Noah had a big job ahead of him! Not only did he need to build a giant ark, but he had to get the animals inside and gather up enough food to last through a giant flood.

Outline
Overview
Bible Story
Opening Game
Object Lesson
Additional Optional Activities

Materials
- **Bibles**
- **Reproducible page 212**
- **Reproducible page 213**
- **Stuffed or toy animals**
- **2 baskets**
- **Favorite toy animal**
- **Measuring tape**
- **Clear Con-Tact paper**
- **White cardstock**
- **Fruit-flavored cereal rings**
- **Glue**
- **Cotton balls**

Opening Game: Animals in the Ark!

Materials

- Stuffed or toy animals
- 2 baskets

Tip: Be sure to evenly disperse the more athletic kids to make things more even.

Preparation: Before class, gather up a number of stuffed or toy animals and place them on one side of the room.

Say: In today's Bible story, God gave Noah some instructions about the animals of the world. He was to gather up two of every kind of animal and bird. Let's pretend we're a part of Noah's family and we have to gather up all the animals.

Directions: Divide the kids into two teams. Place a laundry basket in front of each team. When you say "go", have the kids run to the pile of animals (one by one, relay race style), select an animal, and race back to place it in the laundry basket. Stop the race after one minute. Whichever team has the most animals in their basket at the end of one minute tells a sentence about the Bible story.

DEVELOPMENTAL TIDBITS
School-Aged Children—On the Move

- Their morality moves from what parents do to what they agree with—peers
- Their faith is moving from fiction to fact
- Their faith commitments move from following someone to personal or a peer.
- They are moving from concrete thinkers being capable of understanding more to abstract concepts such as: the Trinity, baptism, and Communion.
- They are moving from only wanting to sense the approval of adults to participating because they are capable of something.
- They are moving from accepting things at face value to questioning.
- They are moving toward needing there to be purpose.

See page 15 for the role of a volunteer in a school-aged child's spiritual journey.

Object Lesson: Favorite Animals

Materials

• Favorite stuffed animal

Tip: If you can, bring in a real animal such as a gerbil or guinea pig. It would really take this lesson over the top. Just be sensitive to any allergies the kids may have.

Say: Do you have a favorite animal? (*Children respond.*)

(*Hold up stuffed animal.*) **This is one of my favorite animals. I sure am glad that God saved this animal during the big flood.** I imagine it was very hard for God to see so many of the things he created being destroyed during the flood. **God does not like sin** and he wanted to get rid of it and start fresh with a family that loved God, Noah's family.

How do you think God felt as everything on Earth was destroyed? (*Children respond.*)

I think you are probably right. After Noah, Noah's family, and the animals were in the ark, God shut the door of the ark. Then, it began to rain. It rained all day and all night for forty days and forty nights (Genesis 7:17).

Have you ever been in a big rainstorm? What was it like? (*Children respond.*)

I wonder if Noah and his family were feeling nervous as they waited for the rains to stop? After a long time, the rain did end and eventually, the water dried up. Noah and all the animals were able to get off the ark. As soon as Noah left the boat, he built an altar to thank God for saving him and his family. God placed a rainbow in the sky as a promise that he would never flood the earth again. Now, whenever you see a rainbow, you can remember God's promise to Noah and the rest of the world.

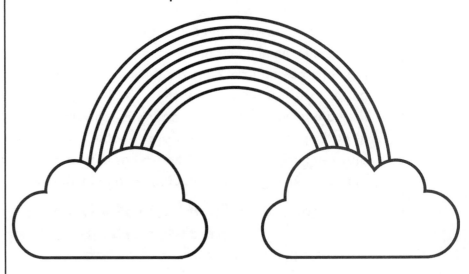

Materials

- Measuring tape

Tip: If you don't have time to measure during class, measure out the ark ahead of time. Use chalk or cones in an outdoor area to mark off the size of the ark.

Materials

- Reproducible page 212
- Clear Con-Tact paper

Bonus Idea: Make a set for each child to take home. Provide a resealable plastic bag to store cards in.

Materials

- Reproducible page 213
- White cardstock
- Fruit-flavored cereal rings
- Glue
- Cotton balls

Measure the Ark

Directions: Break out a measuring tape and stand with the kids at a clear landmark such as a tree or edge of a building. Kids help you measure with the tape to see how long the ark really was.

Say: It is astounding how large the ark really was—500 feet long and 85 feet wide. Let's measure how big the ark would have been to see what an incredible job it was for Noah to build the giant floating vessel. Isn't it incredible that Noah built that all without power tools or a construction crew? No wonder it took anywhere from fifty to seventy-five years for Noah to build the ark!

Animal Memory Game

Preparation: Copy page 212, making one copy for each group of three or four children. Cover animal cards with clear Con-Tact paper and cut apart each set.

Say: Noah brought at least two of every animal onto the ark. Let's play a game to match up animals in sets of two.

Directions: Children divide into groups of three or four. Give each group a set of cards to play Concentration.

Rainbow Colored Cereal Rainbow

Preparation: Photocopy page 213 onto cardstock, making one copy for each child.

Say: God does not like sin, which is why he destroyed the earth with a flood. However, he promised he would never do this again. He gave Noah a rainbow to symbolize this promise.

Directions: Children use their rainbow paper to create a colorful project with the kids. Using fruit flavored cereal rings and tacky glue, create a fruity rainbow. Add cotton balls for clouds.

Chapter 4: Job

BIBLE STORY REFERENCE: Job 1:1–22

MEMORY VERSE: *After Job had prayed for his friends, the Lord restored his fortunes and gave him twice as much as he had before. Job 42:10*

Big Idea
God Is with Us When We Are Sad

Overview

Say: Sometimes life does not go the way we want it to. Sometimes bad things happen and we feel sad or confused about it. There is a book of the Bible that is filled with sad and confusing things. It is the book of Job, and it is the story of a man's life. The man was named Job and he knew that God is with us when we are sad. *(Open with prayer requests, praises, and a time of prayer.)*

Bible Story

Say: Have you ever been sad? What happened? Did anyone help you to feel better? *(Children respond.)*

In today's Bible story, Job had a lot of reasons to be sad. In a very short time, he lost all of his children, his donkeys, camels, and sheep. He was a very sad man. Let's turn in the Bible to Job 1:1–3. *(Read Scripture aloud.)* Now, let's see what happened next. *(Read Job 1:13–22.)*

Job was deeply upset, but he remembered that **God is with us when we are sad.** Job's friends came to him to try and comfort him. *(Read Job 2:11–13.)* **Job suffered greatly.** However, no matter what happened in Job's life, he continued to trust God and remember that God is with us when we are sad.

Outline
Overview
Bible Story
Opening Game
Object Lesson
Additional Optional Activities

Materials
- **Bibles**
- **Small toy animals**
- **Blindfold**
- **Tissues**
- **Three or more tissue boxes**
- **Empty yogurt containers**
- **Rubber bands**
- **Marbles**
- **Cardstock**
- **Markers or crayons**
- **Stickers**

Opening Game: Steal the Cattle

Materials
- Small toy animals
- Chair
- Blindfold

Tip: Instead of toy animals, use cotton balls.

Say: In today's Bible story, Job lost all of his sheep, cattle, and camels. A group of enemies stole all his camels. For this game, we're going to pretend to be the bad guys and steal the camels from Job.

Directions: Place one child in a chair to be Job, facing the wall. Blindfold child or tell them to close their eyes. Place toy animals under the chair.

The other children take turns sneaking up to the chair as quietly as they can to steal an animal. The blindfolded child, "Job," can swing their hands around to the back of the chair when they think they hear someone approaching.

If "Job" catches someone trying to steal an animal, that child is the new "Job." Continue play as time and interest allow.

VOLUNTEER TIDBITS

- What does that mean for the school-aged volunteer?
- Pray for the children, the movement of the Holy Spirit, to be used as an instrument.
- Partner together to make sure the team is on the same page.
- Prepare by studying God's Word, prepare for the lesson and the key learning points.
- Respect the power of peers in the room, but empower the children to think independently.
- Teach the Bible nuts and bolts to the children.
- Promote and Praise each child developing their self-image—Become their number one fan!
- Find real-life application for lessons, modeling and sharing personal (and age-appropriate) stories from your life.
- Challenge their worldview by helping them take ownership of their faith.

See page 16 for Building Blocks of Faith—Infancy Stage.

Object Lesson: Cry It Out

Materials

• Tissues

Tip: Instead of pulling tissues from a box, you could play "Empty that Tissue Box" game from page 17 and save the tissues. You can also use the tissues in the "How Strong Is the Tissue" activity on page 17.

Say: What usually happens when we are sad? (*Children respond.*) That's right! Usually, we cry when we are sad. Then, we need a tissue to blow our nose or wipe our eyes.

When might someone need a box of tissues? When might they be sad? (*Children respond. Hand them a tissue for each answer.*) I think you are probably right. Those are all times when people might be sad. Many of those things happened to Job. He lost his family, many of his favorite things, and he even got very sick. At first, his friends tried to comfort him, but after a while, they started to say some mean things. They hurt his feelings. However, even through all these hard things, Job remembered that **God is with us when we are sad**.

The thing I love about this story is that it does not end with sadness. Let's read about it. (*Read Job 42:10–13, 16–17.*)

Isn't it nice to know that Job was able to be happy again? **God is with us when we are sad** and he is with us when we are happy. He is with us all the time.

DEVELOPMENTAL TIDBITS

Building Blocks of Faith—Each age brings new ability levels of spiritual growth.

Infancy Stage: At this stage, children learn about love, trust and security. This lays the groundwork for them to know that God loves them and they can trust him. They learn that church is safe and other adults are safe.

Turn to page 19 to read about the Building Blocks of Faith—Preschool Stage.

Additional Optional Activities

Materials

- Two or more tissue boxes

Empty that Tissue Box

Say: Now that Job is happy again, maybe we don't need these tissues anymore! Let's see if we can empty the box in under a minute!

Directions: Set a timer for one minute and see if a child can empty out all the tissues from the box before the timer beeps. They must pull the tissues out one by one.

Materials

- Tissues
- Empty yogurt container
- Rubber bands
- Marbles

How Strong Is the Tissue?

Say: How strong do you think a tissue is? Let's try to stack as many marble as we can on this tissue without it breaking.

Directions: In this activity, participants must take a chance on the strength of a tissue. Kids try to place as many marbles on the tissue as possible without breaking through the tissue. Place a tissue over an open container (a large yogurt container works well), and rubber-band in place. Pass out marbles and allow kids to place on tissue, one at a time. Whoever can get the most marbles to stay on top without breaking through says a sentence about the Bible story.

Materials

- Cardstock
- Markers or crayons
- Stickers

Letters of Encouragement

Say: Do you know someone that is currently experiencing a sad time, like Job was? Perhaps a letter of encouragement might help remind them that **God is with us when we are sad**.

Directions: Have kids make their own cards or have some prepared cards available for kids to personalize and send to someone who would be encouraged by them.

Chapter 5: Abraham and God's Promise

BIBLE STORY REFERENCE: Genesis 15:1–6, 21:1–5

MEMORY VERSE: *Now the Lord was gracious to Sarah as he had said, and the Lord did for Sarah what he had promised. Genesis 21:1*

Big Idea
God Keeps His Promises

Overview

Say: After the flood, God continued to work on his plan to save the world from sin. He chose a man, Abraham, to be the father of a special nation called the Israelites. The Israelites would be God's special people. God led Abraham to a new land and promised that Abraham would have many children. However, it did not seem like it would really happen. Abraham had to wait a long time for his promised son, but he learned that God keeps his promises. (*Open with prayer requests, praises, and a time of prayer.*)

Bible Story

Say: Have you ever had to wait a long time for something? Tell me about it. (*Children respond.*)

In today's Bible story, we'll meet a man named Abraham, who was also known as Abraham. God told Abraham that he would have many children, but it did not happen right away. In fact, God told Abraham that he would have as many descendants as the stars in the sky. Let's turn in the Bible to Genesis 15:1–6. (*Read Scripture aloud.*)

Abraham did not have any children when God gave him this promise, but Abraham knew that **God keeps his promises**, so he trusted God and waited for his special child to arrive. After many years, Abraham and his wife Sarah had a baby. (*Read Genesis 21:1–5.*) What an exciting time that must have been!

Outline
Overview
Bible Story
Opening Game
Object Lesson
Additional Optional Activities

Materials
- Bibles
- Reproducible page 214
- 5–10 jars of baby food
- Brown paper bag or tote bag
- Engagement ring
- Fancy ring box
- Cardstock
- Tissue paper
- Glue
- Paint brushes
- Construction paper
- Gift bag
- Baby items
- Baby dolls
- Baby blankets
- Bible-times costumes
- Camera and tripod if available

Opening Game: Sniffing Food

Materials

- 5–10 jars of baby food (peas, bananas, applesauce, green beans, sweet potatoes, etc.)
- Brown paper bag or tote bag

Preparation: Place jars in brown paper bag or tote bag.

Say: Babies eat all kinds of foods when they are a few months old. Today, we're going to try to guess some of the flavors of baby foods.

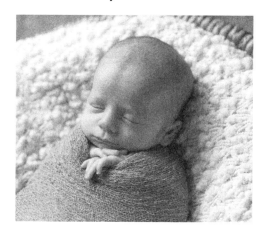

Directions: Kids sit in a circle on the floor. Have everyone close their eyes. Take one jar of baby food out of the bag and quickly remove and hide the label. Remove the lid and move it around the circle, under each child's nose so that each child can smell the food.

Can you guess what kind of baby food this is? If no one guesses, tell children to open their eyes. Children carefully pass the jar around the circle so everyone can see and smell the food again. Continue passing until someone correctly guesses the food.

Repeat the process with the remaining baby food flavors.

DEVELOPMENTAL TIDBITS

Building Blocks of Faith—Each age brings new ability levels of spiritual growth.

Preschool Stage: At this stage, children are open to things they cannot see. Their imagination enables them to believe in a God they cannot see. Trusting adults at church (a stage they mastered at infancy) feeds their need to seek adult connection. They are easily influenced. They are developing their self-image, so hearing how God feels about them at this stage is critical.

Turn to page 24 to read about the Building Blocks of Faith—Elementary Stage.

Object Lesson: Ring-a-Ding

Materials

- Engagement ring
- Fancy ring box

Say: Guess what is inside this fancy box. (*Children respond.*)

If you guessed a ring, you are right! But this isn't just any ring, it's an engagement ring. When does a person usually get an engagement ring? (*Children respond.*)

That's right. Usually when a man wants to marry a woman, he gives her a special ring. If she says, "Yes!" they start to plan a wedding. Do they usually get married right away?

They usually have to wait, and sometimes, for a long time. Sometimes they have to wait to get everything ready or to save up money. Sometimes they have to wait until they finish college. Whatever the reason, they usually have to wait. That is really hard! These two people are very excited about the big day, but it doesn't happen right away. Even though they have to wait, they trust in the promise that this ring symbolizes.

That reminds me of Abraham. God had promised Abraham that he and his wife Sarah would have a son. (*Read Genesis 17:16, 19.*) **He even used the stars to remind Abraham of that special promise.**

How to you think Abraham felt as he waited? (*Children respond.*) Abraham knew that **God keeps his promises,** but it was still hard to wait. Abraham must have been very excited about his baby!

That might be true. Of course, after some time, God did indeed keep his promise to Abraham and Sarah. They had a baby boy and they named him Isaac. They both loved Isaac very much and they were so happy that God keeps his promises.

Materials

- Reproducible page 214
- Cardstock
- Tissue paper, different colors
- Glue
- Paint brushes
- Construction paper cut just smaller than the frame

Family Frame

Preparation: Before class, copy page 214 on cardstock, making one frame for each child. Cut out center of frames. Cut tissue paper into small squares.

Say: God told Abraham that he would have a big family. Let's make a picture frame for a picture of your family.

Directions: Give each child a frame. Place the various colors of tissue paper on the table. Children paint glue onto the frame. Crumble the tissue squares up and place on the glue. To the back of the frames, children glue the construction paper on three of the four sides leaving one side open to slip a picture in.

Materials

- Gift bag
- Baby items (bottle, brush, rattle, teething ring, diaper, pacifier, washcloth, teddy bear, fingernail clippers, shampoo, thermometer, spoon, bib, pack of wipes, shoe, etc)

What's in the Bag?

Say: Abraham and Sarah were so excited about their new bundle of joy! They probably didn't have the same baby stuff that we have today, but we can still play a fun guessing game with some baby items.

Directions: Stock a gift bag or pillowcase with some common baby items. Kids take turns putting their hand into the bag (without looking), feeling an item and guessing what it is.

Materials

- Baby dolls
- Baby blankets
- Bible-times costumes
- Camera and tripod, if available

Family Pictures

Say: Abraham and Sarah didn't have the option of getting family pictures, but we can pretend! Let's use the props and pretend we're Abraham and Sarah taking a family photo.

Directions: Set up a station with baby dolls, baby boy clothes, blankets, Bible costumes, and maybe even a few wigs and fake beards. Next to this, set up a tripod with a camera or camera phone. Encourage the kids to dress up as Abraham and Sarah and then take pictures with their new baby boy. Expect things to get a little silly.

Chapter 6: Isaac and His Sons

BIBLE STORY REFERENCE: Genesis 25:19–34

MEMORY VERSE: *Bear with each other and forgive one another if any of you has a grievance against someone. Forgive as the Lord forgave you.* Colossians 3:13

**Big Idea
I Can Choose Forgiveness**

Overview

Say: Abraham's son Isaac grew up and got married. Isaac and his wife, Rebekah, had twin boys named Jacob and Esau. Jacob and Esau did not have a good relationship growing up. At one point, Jacob even ran away from home because Esau was so angry at him. Many years later, Jacob and Esau met again. Esau could have continued to be angry at Jacob, but he learned that I can choose forgiveness. Jacob and Esau were able to be friends because Esau chose forgiveness. (*Open with prayer requests, praises, and a time of prayer.*)

Bible Story

Say: Have you ever been really mad at someone? Did you choose to forgive them? (*Children respond.*)

Our Bible story today is about twin brothers. Even though they were twins, they were very different. Let's turn in the Bible to Genesis 25. (*Read Genesis 25:27–28.*) **One day, Esau came in from the field and was so hungry that he made a foolish decision.** (*Read Genesis 25:29–34.*) **Later, when it came time for Isaac, the twin boys' father to die, Jacob wanted to make sure he got the birthright instead of Esau. Let's read what happened.** (*Read Genesis 27:5–10.*) **Esau was so angry when he found out what happened that he wanted to kill his own brother.** (*Read Genesis 27:41.*) **But Jacob ran away. Years later, Jacob returned home, afraid of how his brother would feel about him. But when Jacob was still on the road, Esau traveled to meet him. Esau had chosen to forgive his brother! He was no longer angry with Jacob.**

Outline
**Overview
Bible Story
Opening Game
Object Lesson
Additional Optional Activities**

Materials
- **Bibles**
- **Reproducible page 215**
- **Glass of milk**
- **Lemon juice**
- **Cooking pot**
- **Vegetable broth**
- **Ladle**
- **Bowls**
- **Spices**
- **Precut vegetables**
- **Spoons**
- **Napkins**
- **Paper**
- **Art supplies**
- **Markers or crayons**
- **Heart stickers**

Opening Game: What Are You Feeling?

Directions: Instruct children to act out the emotions during this review of the story with the following motions:

Happy = clap your hands

Mad = stomp feet and shake fists

Scared = put hands on face and say "oh no!"

Sad = rub eyes or pretend to cry

Say: Esau gave away his birthright—his inheritance—for a bowl of stew. Later, Jacob tricked their father into giving him Esau's birthright and blessing. Let's review the story together. I'll read a sentence and with the motions above, act out how you think that person was feeling.

- Isaac told Esau to make him a meal. At the meal, Isaac would give Esau a blessing.

- Rebekah, the twin's mother, overhead this and told Jacob how to trick his father.

- Isaac could not see well, so he gave away the blessing to Jacob without truly knowing it was him.

- When Esau returned from hunting, he discovered that his blessing and birthright were gone.

- Rebekah told Jacob to run away. Jacob went to his uncle's house far away.

- Jacob lived with his uncle a long time, got married, and had many children. After many years, God told Jacob to return to his own home.

- When Jacob was near to meeting Esau, he sent gifts for Esau and prayed that God would protect him.

- When Esau and Jacob met, Esau hugged Jacob. Esau chose forgiveness. He was no longer angry at Jacob.

Object Lesson: Lemony Milk

Materials

- Glass of milk
- Lemon juice

Say: Who likes milk around here? When do you like to drink milk? (*Children respond.*)

I love drinking milk right after I have eaten a cookie. It's so refreshing. Would any one like a sip of this milk here? (*Check for allergies, and allow a volunteer to take a sip.*) **What do you think? Pretty tasty?**

This milk is pretty delicious, but what do you think would happen if I poured some of this lemon juice into the milk? (*Children respond. Pour some of the lemon juice into the milk and show the kids how the lemon juice makes the milk curdle.*)

This lemon juice is like anger and bitterness and the milk is like our hearts. When we let anger sit in our hearts, it starts to turn our hearts sour. Does anyone want a sip of this milk now? (*Even if they say yes, do not let the kids drink!*)

You would not want to drink this milk because it is sour and gross now. (*Kids look at the milk and maybe smell it.*) When we remember that we can choose forgiveness, we don't let our hearts turn sour. It's not always easy to forgive, but God will help us do it. Just like Esau forgave his brother Jacob after all those years, **we can choose forgiveness** for the people in our lives as well.

DEVELOPMENTAL TIDBITS

Building Blocks of Faith—Each age brings new ability levels of spiritual growth.

Elementary Stage: At this stage, children begin to move from the literal to being able to understand the abstract. They are moving from fantasy to wanting more facts. Peers are becoming a bigger influence on them. Encouraging good friendships is important. They are rapidly forming their self-image. Spending time affirming them helps them sense their worth to you and God. This is the age they are most likely to make a faith commitment. Provide opportunities for them to hear the salvation message. They want to feel a sense of purpose. "Just because" is not an effective answer to questions. They need to know the why to the things of God. Help them develop a firm foundation to defend their faith.

Turn to page 27 for Stages of Faith.

Materials

- Cooking pot
- Vegetable broth
- Ladle
- Bowls
- Spices
- Precut vegetables
- Spoons
- Napkins

Tip: If you don't have access to a stove, use a microwave to cook the soup.

Allergy Alert: Post a sign with a list of ingredients for parents to see when they drop-off their children.

Materials

- Paper
- Art supplies

Materials

- Reproducible page 215
- Markers or crayons
- Heart stickers

Making Stew

Preparation: Pour broth into cooking pot and heat until hot. Place cut vegetables and spices on a table.

Say: Jacob was making delicious stew one day when Esau came in from the fields. Jacob's stew was so delicious that Esau traded his birthright for it. Let's make some tasty stew as well!

Directions: Ladle broth into a bowl for each child. Children then add vegetables and spices to their broth to make a stew. Give children spoons and napkins to use while enjoying their snack.

Art Therapy

Say: Just like Esau, **we can choose forgiveness**. Is there something you are feeling angry about? Something you're feeling sorry for? Or maybe you're just feeling happy! Draw a picture about how you are feeling. While you draw, pray, asking God to help you forgive if you need to forgive, or ask for courage to ask forgiveness, if that's what you need to do.

Directions: This lesson may have reminded kids of someone they need to forgive. Provide art supplies for kids to draw a picture to pray about.

Sorry Cards

Say: Do you need to say sorry to someone like Jacob did? Let's make a card to say sorry and give it to the person you hurt. Or save the card for the next time you need to say "sorry" to someone.

Preparation: Copy page 215, making one copy for each child.

Directions: Children decorate reproducible page to make an apology card.

Chapter 7: Jacob's Twelve Sons

BIBLE STORY REFERENCE: Genesis 37:4–28

MEMORY VERSE: [Jacob] *loved Joseph more than any of his other sons, because he had been born to him in his old age; and he made an ornate robe for him. Genesis 37:3*

**Big Idea
God Loves All His Children**

Overview

Say: Jacob had many children as he got older. In fact, he had twelve sons! Jacob loved one son more than any of his other sons, and this caused a lot of problems with the family. The son that Jacob loved the best was Joseph. He even made Joseph a beautiful fancy robe. This made his brothers very mad and very jealous.

The Bible tells us that we can become children of God (Galatians 3:26 and John 1:12) if we believe in God and accept his free gift of salvation. **God loves all his children** and he does not want us to fight the way Jacob's sons did. (*Open with prayer requests, praises, and a time of prayer.*)

Bible Story

Say: Do you ever have trouble getting along with your brothers or sisters? (*Children respond.*)

In our Bible story today, Joseph had a hard time getting along with his brothers. His brothers did not like that Joseph got special gifts, and they did not like hearing about his dreams. Let's read about it. (*Read Genesis 37:4–5.*) The brothers got so mad at Joseph, that one day, they did something terrible. Let's read what happened in Genesis 37:26–28. (*Read Scripture aloud.*) Joseph was taken away from his home because his brothers were jealous that he was the favorite. Unlike Jacob, **God loves all his children.** We are all special to him.

Outline
Overview
Bible Story
Opening Game
Object Lesson
Additional Optional Activities

Materials
• Bibles
• Reproducible page 216
• Reproducible page 217
• Bathrobes
• Variety of wrapped candies
• Fabric scraps
• Glue
• 12 index cards
• Markers or crayons
• Yarn or twine
• Craft sticks
• Scissors

Opening Game: Robe Relay

Materials

- Bathrobes, one for each team of three or four

Tip: It may help to have them touch a wall or cone at the point where they turn around to return to the finish line.

Preparation: Collect bathrobes from family and friends. You should have one robe for every three or four players. Use masking tape to make start and finish lines at each end of the playing area.

Say: Joseph was given a very colorful coat or robe by his father. In this game, we're going to wear a robe as well in order to run in the race.

Directions: Divide kids into teams based on the number of robes. Teams line up at start line. Hand the first player on each team a robe.

On your signal, the first child in each line puts on robe, runs to the finish line and returns to the starting line.

Player removes the robe and hands it to the next player in line who then repeats the process.

After completing their leg of the race, children cheer on their teammates. First team to finish tells a sentence about the Bible story.

DEVELOPMENTAL TIDBITS
Stages of Faith Development

Faith development is continual resizing and reinvention.

Children crave a faith that's understandable, relevant, and applicable. They want a faith that doesn't wear out. Successful completion of each stage looks like:

Stage 1: I need to believe that I am loved unconditionally. If I become certain of God's forgiveness I am able to shed my wrong self-image and receive God's healing.

Stage 2: God the Father—I must replace misinformation and ideas about God and replace them with biblical truth. I need to trust God and allow him to repair my distorted ideas.

Turn to page 31 for Stages 3 and 4.

Object Lesson: Candy Time

Materials

- Variety of wrapped candies

Tip: Be sensitive to families that don't want their children to eat sweets. Provide a substitute for those children.

Say: Wow! Look at all this delicious candy. Does anyone want a piece? (*Assure kids that everyone will get a piece.*)

Directions: Select a volunteer and tell them to pick their favorite candy. After they have done so, select two more volunteers and tell them to pick their favorite candy. Allow volunteers to return to their seats, but ask them not to eat candy yet.

Say: It seems like everyone has a favorite type of candy. I personally love (*Name your favorite candy.*). It's not a big deal when we have a favorite candy because it doesn't really hurt anyone to have a favorite candy. But in our Bible story, Jacob had a favorite son and it caused a lot of trouble for the family.

What kind of trouble did picking a FAVORITE son cause for Jacob's family? (*Children respond.*)

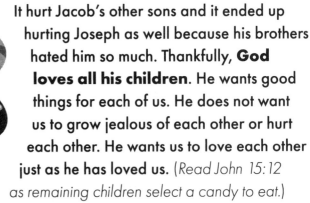

It hurt Jacob's other sons and it ended up hurting Joseph as well because his brothers hated him so much. Thankfully, **God loves all his children**. He wants good things for each of us. He does not want us to grow jealous of each other or hurt each other. He wants us to love each other just as he has loved us. (*Read John 15:12 as remaining children select a candy to eat.*)

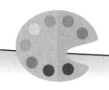

Additional Optional Activities

Materials
- Reproducible page 216
- Fabric scraps
- Glue

Tip: Ask your congregation to donate fabric scraps, check thrift stores for fabric or old tablecloths and bed linens, or check the remnant bin at fabrics stores. Construction paper can also be used if fabric is not available.

Materials
- 12 index cards
- Markers or crayons

Tip: For durability, laminate cards or cover with clear packing tape or Con-Tact paper.

Materials
- Reproducible page 217
- Yarn or twine
- Craft sticks, two for each child
- Markers or crayons
- Scissors

Coat of Many Colors

Preparation: Copy page 216, making one for each child.

Say: Jacob gave his favorite son Joseph a coat of many colors. Let's glue on colorful fabric to make a robe like Joseph's.

Directions: Kids glue fabric scraps on their paper to make a robe of many colors.

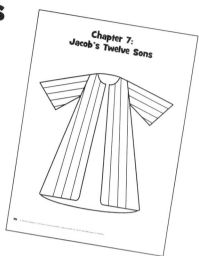

Chapter 7:
Jacob's Twelve Sons

Where Are the Brothers?

Preparation: Using index cards, make a set of twelve cards, each with a drawing of one Jacob's twelve sons (simple stick figures will do!). Label each card with one son's name (Reuben, Simon, Levi, Judah, Dan, Naphtali, Gad, Asher, Issachar, Zebulun, Joseph, Benjamin). Hide cards throughout the room.

Say: Jacob has twelve sons! That is a lot to keep track of! Let's work together as a group and find the sons who are hidden throughout this room.

Directions: Kids search to find cards for Jacob's twelve sons.

Sun, Moon, and Stars Mobile

Preparation: Copy page 217, making one for each child.

Say: Joseph had a dream that the sun, moon, and stars were bowing down to him. Let's make a craft to remind us of Joseph's dream.

Directions: Give kids two craft sticks and some yarn or twine. Children cross craft sticks over each other to form an X and secure in place with yarn. Hang yarn from each of the four ends of the craft sticks. Children color, cut out, and attach sun, moon, and stars. Make a loop in the center of the X for hanging the mobile.

Chapter 8: Joseph in Egypt

BIBLE STORY REFERENCE: *Genesis 41:9–27, 42:1–8, 45:1–8*

MEMORY VERSE: *You intended to harm me, but God intended it for good to accomplish what is now being done, the saving of many lives. Genesis 50:20*

Big Idea
God Sees the Big Picture

Overview

Say: Joseph was hated by his brothers. They hated him so much, in fact, that they sold him to a group of traveling merchants. Joseph was taken to Egypt and became a slave in a man named Potiphar's house. Many difficult things happened in Joseph's life, but Joseph continued to trust God. Even when things don't make sense, **God sees the big picture**. God had a plan for Joseph's life and God has a plan for our life as well. (*Open with prayer requests, praises, and a time of prayer.*)

Bible Story

Say: After Joseph was taken to Egypt, he served in Potiphar's house. Joseph worked hard and was soon in charge of the whole house. One day, Potiphar's wife told lies about Joseph, and Joseph was sent to prison. Joseph still trusted God and tried to help others. With God's help, he told other prisoners what their dreams meant. One day, Pharaoh had a strange dream. (*Read Genesis 41:9–27.*) Joseph was put in charge of storing grain for Egypt. One day, Joseph's own brothers came to Egypt because they had no food! (*Read Genesis 42:1–8.*) Joseph wanted to see if his brothers were sorry about what they did to him. When he realized that they were sorry, he revealed who he was. (*Read Genesis 45:1–8.*) Joseph knew that **God sees the big picture** and coming to Egypt was part of God's plan.

Outline
Overview
Bible Story
Opening Game
Object Lesson
Additional Optional Activities

Materials
- Bibles
- Reproducible page 218
- Everyday objects
- Camera or cell phone
- Printer
- Jigsaw puzzle
- Scarf or towel
- Rice
- Measuring cup or scoop
- Small buckets
- Old pieces from various puzzles
- Glue
- Cardstock
- Name tags
- Pencils
- Markers

Opening Game: What is it?

Materials

- Everyday objects (tape dispenser, toothbrush, handle on drawer, fork, carpet, grass, spool of thread, spiral binding on notebook, button, candy, leaf, playground equipment, toys, jewelry, and a crayon)
- Camera or cell phone
- Printer

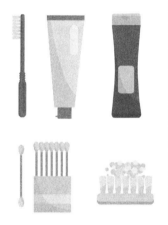

Preparation: Print several pictures of everyday objects. Zoom in on the objects very close so it is hard to tell what the object is. Then, take a regular picture of the object so kids can see what it is. Print (or have the pictures developed) and then pair pictures up.

Directions: Hold up the close-up picture first and see if the kids can guess what the object is. Then, show them the regular picture.

Say: Sometimes it's hard to tell what something is when we are really close to it—like in our game when we tried to identify the close-up pictures. **God sees the big picture** and he can always make sense of things, but sometimes it's hard for us to understand. It must have been hard for Joseph as he lived in Egypt, but through his story, we can remember that **God sees the big picture** and has a plan for each of our lives.

DEVELOPMENTAL TIDBITS

Stage 3: I need to experience mutual support and challenging relationships that can be found in the family of God in order to grow spiritually.

Stage 4: My faith –I need to develop ownership of my personal faith. As my personal faith grows I can move away from the need to be like my peers and rely on biblical principles.

Turn to page 32 for Stages 5 and 6.

Object Lesson: Puzzling Picture

Materials

- Jigsaw puzzle
- Scarf or towel

Preparation: Assemble puzzle on a table in your classroom. Remove one piece and place on table away from the puzzle. Cover puzzle with scarf or towel.

Say: Who likes puzzles? What's the hardest part? Is it easier to do a puzzle if you know what the final picture is supposed to be?

Directions: Hold up the last pieces and encourage the kids to guess what the final picture might be for that particular puzzle.

Say: It's pretty hard to tell what the whole puzzle is supposed to look like based on just one piece, isn't it? This puzzle piece is a lot like a day in our life. By itself, it doesn't make much sense. Sometimes we can see that it's a part of something bigger, but not always. We can only really see a small piece, but **God sees the big picture.**

(*Uncover puzzle and put the last piece in place.*) **Is the picture what you thought it might be? Touch your nose if you were surprised by the completed puzzle.**

No matter what is happening, **God sees the big picture** of each of our lives. He has a plan for us. He had a plan for Joseph. When Joseph first came to Egypt, he was a slave. He even spent some time in prison for a crime he did not commit. But because he trusted God and always tried to do the right thing, eventually God allowed him to become a great ruler in Egypt. (*Read Genesis 41:14–16, 39.*) **Because of this, Joseph was able to see his brothers again, give them food during a great famine, and reunite his family.**

DEVELOPMENTAL TIDBITS

Stage 5: I grow as I allow God's Word to change me. I understand the need to allow the Holy Spirit to change me as I seek God's truth for my life. The Bible has a centering and guiding influence on me.

Stage 6: I understand that there is evil at work against me, the world, flesh, devil. I am willing to make a stand against this with the help of God and the Holy Spirit.

Turn to page 35 for Stages 7 and 8.

Additional Optional Activities

Materials

- Rice
- Measuring cup or scoop, one for each team of four or five
- Small buckets, one for each team of four or five plus one more

Fill Up the Grain Bags

Preparation: Place rice in one of the buckets and place on one side of the playing area.

Say: In our Bible story today, Pharaoh had two dreams with the same meaning. Joseph's job was to store up the grain for when Egypt would need it. In this game, you must gather grain, being careful not to waste any.

Directions: Kids line up in teams opposite the bucket of rice, relay race style. When the race starts, one child from each team will run to the other side of the room to the small bucket of rice. Using a measuring cup, they scoop up a cup of rice and return to the starting line, being careful to not spill (speed is not the goal!). They will dump rice into a waiting empty team bucket and pass the measuring cup to the next child in line. After everyone has had a chance to "race," the buckets can be weighed to see who has the most grain or rice.

Materials

- Old pieces from various puzzles
- Glue
- Cardstock

God Sees the Big Picture

Say: We see one piece of our life at a time, but **God sees the big picture**. Let's make a craft that will remind us of our lesson.

Directions: Using puzzle pieces from old puzzles, create a craft that reminds kids that **God sees the big picture**. Using a piece of cardstock as a base, glue puzzle pieces all around the perimeter of the paper. In the middle, have the kids write, "God Sees the Big Picture" along with today's Bible story reference.

Materials

- Reproducible page 218
- Name tags, one for each child
- Pencils
- Markers

Hieroglyphic Name Tag

Preparation: Copy page 218, making one for each child.

Say: The Egyptians wrote with hieroglyphics which are both fun to look at and use. Let's write like the Egyptians by writing our names.

Directions: Using the chart provided, kids use a pencil to write their name in hieroglyphics on a name tag. When done, children go back over the pencil marks with a marker to make permanent.

Chapter 9: Baby Moses Is Saved

BIBLE STORY REFERENCE: Genesis 6:5–19

MEMORY VERSE: *When the child grew older, she took him to Pharaoh's daughter and he became her son. She named him Moses, saying, "I drew him out of the water." Exodus 2:10*

Big Idea
God Has a Plan for Every Person

Overview

Say: After Joseph was reunited with his brothers, his whole family moved to Egypt. They lived a long time and had many children. They were called Hebrews or the Israelites. After many years, a new Pharaoh became king who did not remember the great things Joseph had done. He did not like the Israelites and decided to do something awful. (*Open with prayer requests, praises, and a time of prayer.*)

Bible Story

Say: Have you ever imagined what it would be like to be a prince or princess? What do you think the best part would be? (*Children respond.*)

In our Bible story today, Moses became a prince of Egypt when he was just a baby. The king of Egypt, Pharaoh, did not like that there were so many Israelites. He was afraid that one day, they might decide to start a war against the Egyptians. So Pharaoh commanded that all the baby boys be thrown into the Nile River. Let's hear what one woman did when she heard this command. (*Read Exodus 2:1–10.*) **God has a plan for every person** and he had a plan for Moses. Moses was saved and taken into the palace to be raised as royalty. Someday Moses would grow up to be a great leader of God's people.

Outline
Overview
Bible Story
Opening Game
Object Lesson
Additional Optional Activities

Materials
- **Bibles**
- **Reproducible page 219**
- **Small toy person**
- **Postcards from vacations or trips**
- **1-inch construction-paper strips**
- **Construction paper sheets**
- **Transparent tape**
- **Green and brown construction paper**
- **Blue tissue paper**
- **Glue**

Opening Game: Where Is Moses?

Materials

- Small toy person

Say: Moses' mother hid him in a basket and put him in the Nile River in order to keep him safe from Pharaoh. In this game, you are going to try to guess who is hiding baby Moses.

Directions: Children sit in a circle facing each other and close their eyes. Quietly hand one child a small toy person and have them hide it in their lap. Children open their eyes. Pick a volunteer to guess "who is hiding baby Moses." Choose up to three guessers. If no one guesses correctly, the person who has the toy person reveals it to the group. Play again as time permits.

DEVELOPMENTAL TIDBITS

Stage 7: I understand that I am part of an ultimate plan. God uses me to impact others in God's family as well as those around me in the world. Not only are they to help me, but I am to influence and nurture them in their spiritual journey.

Stage 8: My goal is to end well and going strong. Seeing my place as a sage of wisdom and experience, I continue on to regularly develop and nurture others in their faith walk. As I do this, I will continue to nurture a deepening relationship with God.

Turn to page 39 for more Developmental Tidbits.

Object Lesson: Family Vacations

Materials

- Postcards from vacations or trips

Say: Have you ever taken a special trip with your family? Did someone plan the trip? Were there any surprises for you on the trip? (*Pause after each questions for children to respond.*)

Often, when families go on a vacation or on a special trip, there is a lot of planning that happens. You need to plan where to drive, where to stay, where to eat, and what you want to see when you are on your trip.

Directions: Show the kids some of the postcards you brought, sharing the things you planned on and the things you did in each place.

Say: In our Bible story today, Moses' mom did something a little crazy. She knew that baby Moses was not safe at her house, so she put him in a basket and set him in the river. Let's read about it. (*Read Exodus 2:1–4.*)

Moses' mother did not really have a plan for Moses, but we know that **God has a plan for each one of us.** Imagine Moses' mother's surprise when Moses was taken in by the princess of Egypt. The princess even asked Moses' mother to help with the baby for a little while!

Later, when Moses was older, God helped him to become a great leader. Eventually, Moses would help save his people from the evil Pharaoh and free them from the country of Egypt.

I bet Moses' mother would have never guessed that would happen. God has a plan for each person and this was his plan for Moses all along. Just like God had a plan for Moses, **God has a plan for each one of us.** We might be really surprised at how things end up along the way!

Additional Optional Activities

Materials

- 1-inch construction-paper strips
- Construction paper sheets
- Transparent tape

Materials

- Green and brown construction paper
- Blue tissue paper
- Glue

Materials

- None

Tip: The baby games from Chapter 5: Abraham and God's Promise could easily be adapted for this lesson as well.

Basket Weaving

Say: Basket weaving was very common in Egypt. Let's do our own simple version of basket weaving with some construction paper.

Directions: Cut one sheet of construction paper into strips lengthwise, stopping just before the end. Use the first strips to weave in and out on the cut paper, securing the ends with tape.

Down by the River

Say: Moses was found by Pharaoh's daughter in the Nile River. Let's make our own version of the river with construction paper and tissue paper.

Directions: Using green and brown construction paper for the reeds and blue tissue paper for the river, kids can recreate the Nile scene from Egypt. Glue the bottom of the reeds about halfway down the page. Then, cover with the tissue paper to make the reeds look like they are submerged under water.

Who Is Crying?

Say: The princess found baby Moses because he was crying. Let's play a game where you will cry like a baby, too.

Directions: Kids will sit with their heads down on the table. Quietly pick one child, who will then "cry like a baby." After they are done crying, everyone opens their eyes and sits up. Kids must guess who the crying baby was.

Turn to page 219 for a bonus activity

Chapter 10: Moses and Pharaoh

BIBLE STORY REFERENCE: Exodus 7:20–21; 8:1–4, 24; 9:23–26; 10:21–22

MEMORY VERSE: *The Lord said to Moses, "Now you will see what I will do to Pharaoh: Because of my mighty hand he will let them go; because of my mighty hand he will drive them out of his country." Exodus 6:1*

Overview

Say: Pharaoh did not like God's people, the Israelites. He forced them to be slaves and treated them with cruelness. The people prayed and asked God to save them. God had saved Moses for just this reason. By God's power, Moses was to free the people from Egypt. (*Open with prayer requests, praises, and a time of prayer.*)

Bible Story

Say: Who is the strongest person you know? What kind of things can they do? (*Children respond.*)

Pharaoh was a powerful man. He was the ruler over all of Egypt. Many of the Egyptians even believed that he was a god. We know that God is the only true god! And **God is stronger than any man.** In today's Bible story, both the Egyptians and the Israelites see how strong God really is. At first, Moses was afraid to go see Pharaoh, but God told Moses that he would be with him. (*Read Exodus 3:12.*) When Pharaoh refused to let God's people go, God sent plagues on the land of Egypt. Let's read about some of them. (*Read 7:20–21; 8:1–4, 24; 9:23–26; 10:21–22.*) Finally, Pharaoh realized that **God is stronger than any man** and he let God's people go free.

Outline
Overview
Bible Story
Opening Game
Object Lesson
Additional Optional Activities

Materials
- Bibles
- Reproducible page 220
- Balance scale
- Two toy people
- Small weights or stones
- Building blocks
- Children's Bible
- Camera and tripod
- Children's book about Egypt
- Pillows and/or bean-bag chairs

Materials

- Reproducible page 220

Preparation: Copy and cut out the flashcards on page 220.

Say: A lot of crazy things happened in Egypt after Pharaoh refused to let God's people go. God wanted to show that he is stronger than any man, so he sent ten plagues to Egypt. In this game, we're going to act out those plagues. You must listen closely and act quickly! The last person to move sits down for the rest of the round.

Directions: Select a flashcard and call out a plague to the kids. Everyone acts it out in some way. You can make up motions ahead of time to increase the difficulty or have kids make up their own motions. The last child to act out the plague sits down. You can switch between plagues as quickly as you want. Kids will soon be falling all over themselves trying to act like frogs, flies, or dying cattle.

DEVELOPMENTAL TIDBITS
School-Aged Tidbits

- Morality moves from agreeing with their parents just because they are their parents to what they agree with—peers.
- Faith is moving from fantasy to fact based.
- Faith commitments move from following adult influence to their own personal view or the view of a peer.
- School-aged children are moving from "Can do" attitude to their perception of their ability.

Turn to page 43 for more Developmental Tidbits.

Object Lesson: Pharaoh's Power

MATERIALS

- Balance scale
- Two toy people
- Small weights or stones

Say: Pharaoh was a very powerful man. He ruled all of Egypt and everyone did exactly what he said. Of course, we know God is stronger than any man and through the plagues, God showed he was much more powerful than Pharaoh. (*Put one person figure on each side of the scale.*)

- **Pharaoh was strong.** (*Put one stone with the Pharaoh figure.*)

- **He had servants and slaves.** (*Put one stone with the Pharaoh figure.*)

- **He had magicians that could perform amazing tricks.** (*Put one stone with the Pharaoh figure.*)

- **He had armies and chariots.** (*Put one stone with the Pharaoh figure. Kids to observe how much stronger Pharaoh seemed than Moses.*)

- **But, Moses had a secret weapon. God was on Moses' side. God told Moses that He would be with him.** (*Read Exodus 3:12.*)

- **And God is stronger than any man. God is strong.** (*Put one stone with the Moses figure.*)

- **God made all the people in the world.** (*Put two stones with the Moses figure.*)

- **God created the entire world and can control everything in it.** (*Put three stones with the Moses figure.*)

- **He can cause earthquakes and storms.** (*Put two stones with the Moses figure.*)

- **God has power over life and death.** (*Put two stones with the Moses figure.*)

- **Pharaoh may have been strong, but God is stronger than any man.**

Additional Optional Activities

Materials
- Building blocks

Materials
- Children's Bible
- Camera and tripod, if available

Materials
- Children's book about Egypt
- Pillows and/or bean-bag chairs

Building Egypt

Say: The Israelites were forced to do a lot of hard labor, including building large structures like the pyramids. Let's try to build some things that we might see in Egypt.

Directions: Children use building blocks to build things that they might see in Egypt. Pyramids are a great project to start with.

Movie Reenactment

Say: Let's imagine we were a part of the Bible story. As I read through the story, act out what you hear.

Directions: Using a Children's Bible, read through plagues of Egypt (Exodus 7–13). As you read, encourage the kids to act out the story. You may want to assign specific roles such as Moses, Pharaoh, Aaron, Pharaoh's officials, the Israelites, and the Egyptians. If the kids seem to especially enjoy the activity, set up a camera and tripod and record the reenactment. If time permits, watch video together as a group.

All About Egypt

Preparation: Borrow some picture books from the library about Egypt. Set up a comfortable space in the corner of the room with pillows and/or bean bag chairs.

Say: The Israelites would have experienced the things found in these books. Take a look and see what you can find!

Directions: Kids relax and look at books.

Chapter 11: Israelites in the Desert

BIBLE STORY REFERENCE: Exodus 14:10–14, 21–22

MEMORY VERSE: *The Lord will fight for you; you need only to be still. Exodus 14:14*

Big Idea
God Can Do Impossible Things

Overview

Say: Pharaoh let God's people go! Now, the Israelites were headed to the desert to worship the one true God. But it wasn't long before Pharaoh changed his mind. Pharaoh gathered his armies and his chariots and went after the Israelites. The Israelites were stuck with the Red Sea in front of them and Pharaoh's army behind them. They were scared! **God can do impossible things**, and he was about to save them in an amazing way.

(Open with prayer requests, praises, and a time of prayer.)

Bible Story

Say: Have you ever been swimming in a lake, pond, or ocean? What happens when you put your hand down through the water? *(Children respond.)*

Water is an interesting thing. You can't really make a hole in it or split it up. It just runs back together. In today's Bible story, we see that God can do impossible things. Let's read about impossible things God did. *(Read Exodus 14:10–14 and 21–22.)* Wow! God did a lot of other impossible things while the Israelites traveled through the desert, including making bread fall from heaven (Exodus 16), making water come out of a rock (Exodus 17), **causing the ground to open up** (Numbers 16), **and** healing the people from poisonous snake bites (Numbers 21). God stayed with the people and led them throughout the desert with a giant cloud during the day and a pillar of fire at night. The Israelites surely knew that **God can do impossible things.**

Outline
Overview
Bible Story
Opening Game
Object Lesson
Additional Optional Activities

Materials
- Bibles
- Reproducible page 221
- Objects for an obstacle course
- Eggs
- Bowl
- Sand paper
- Blue paper
- Glue
- Fish stickers
- Video clip of the Israelites crossing the Red Sea
- Cardstock
- Markers
- Glue
- Scissors
- Craft sticks

Opening Game: Through the Red Sea

Materials

- Objects for an obstacle course (cones, ropes, chairs, piles of books, blankets, etc.)

Optional: Time each child to see how fast they can "run through the river."

Bonus Idea: If the course is too easy, have kids carry clothing, baskets, or bundles of blankets (like the Israelites did) as they race.

Preparation: Use objects to set up a simple obstacle course.

Say: The Israelites were probably hurrying through the Red Sea. They didn't know how close Pharaoh was behind them. And even though there was no water in their way, there may have been rocks and other obstacles. Today, we're going to pretend we're the Israelites and race through the Red Sea.

Directions: Children take turns running through the obstacle course.

DEVELOPMENTAL TIDBITS
School-Aged Tidbits

School-aged children are moving
- From concrete (literal) thinking to abstract thinking. Concepts like the Trinity, baptism, and Communion can be grasped.
- From their preschool stage of seeking approval from adults to participating for their own reasons: because they are good at the task, are wanted by their peers, want to learn, etc.
- From accepting what they hear at face value to questioning everything.
- Toward needing a purpose or a reason for what they are asked to do or believe.

Turn to page 44 for more Developmental Tidbits.

Object Lesson: Impossible Egg Breaking

Materials
- Eggs
- Bowl

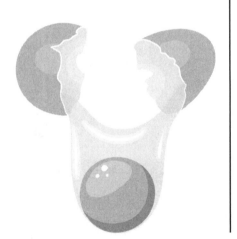

Say: Who thinks they can break this egg by squeezing it in just one hand?

Directions: A volunteer comes forward and tries to break the egg by squeezing it with one hand. Hold over a bowl—just in case! If you have time, let two or three kids try.

Say: This seems like a pretty easy task, but apparently, it's impossible to do!

Do you think God could break this egg with just one hand? (*Children respond.*) Of course he could, because God can do impossible things. God could break this egg and he can do lots of other impossible things.

What kind of impossible things can you think of that God can do? (*Children respond.*)

It's exciting to know that **God can do impossible things.** In our Bible story today, God did something impossible. Let's check it out. (*Read Exodus 14:10–31.*)

That sounds like a pretty impossible thing! God is powerful and amazing and he did many impossible things for the Israelites. He continues to do impossible things for his people today!

Directions: As time allows, other kids to try the egg experiment.

DEVELOPMENTAL TIDBITS
What Are They Capable Of?

- Able to use their Bible and memorize
- Learn how to study the Bible—different sections
- Starting to grasp abstract concepts—baptism, Communion, Trinity, Holy Spirit
- Praying with understanding and purpose
- Personal Bible study, personal application

Turn to page 47 for more Developmental Tidbits.

Additional Optional Activities

Materials

- Sand paper
- Blue paper
- Glue
- Fish stickers

Splitting the Red Sea

Say: When the Israelites crossed the Red Sea, they saw that God can do impossible things. Let's make a craft that will remind us of the lesson today.

Directions: In this craft, the "dry ground" is made with sand paper, giving a memorable textured feel. To begin, give each child a piece of blue paper and a strip of sand paper. Have them glue the sandpaper down the middle of the "sea." They can add waves to the sea or fish stickers.

Materials

- Video clip of Israelites crossing the Red Sea

Tip: Select a clip from a movie that depicts the Israelites crossing the Red Sea. A good choice might be *The Prince of Egypt* which is available at many libraries. You can also find a clip online by searching for "prince of Egypt parting and crossing the Red Sea."

Show a Clip

Say: Can you imagine what it would have been like to cross the sea like the Israelites? Let's watch this movie clip to give us an idea.

Directions: Show the video clip of the Israelites crossing the Red Sea.

Materials

- Reproducible page 221
- Cardstock
- Markers
- Glue
- Scissors
- Craft stick

Enrichment Idea: Add glitter to the fire to help it look like it is sparkling.

Cloud by Day, Fire by Night

Preparation: Print page 221 on cardstock, making one for each child.

Say: God led his people in a very special way through the desert. Let's make a pillar that shows both the cloud (daylight) and fire (night) that God used to guide the Israelites.

Directions: Children color the fire red and yellow, glue cotton balls to the cloud and cut out shapes. Children glue the fire and the cloud back to back, slipping a craft stick in between them at the bottom.

Chapter II: Israelites in the Desert

Chapter 12: Jericho

BIBLE STORY REFERENCE: Joshua 6:2–20

MEMORY VERSE: *When the trumpets sounded, the army shouted, and at the sound of the trumpet, when the men gave a loud shout, the wall collapsed; so everyone charged straight in, and they took the city. Joshua 6:20*

**Big Idea
We Can Always Trust God**

Overview

Say: After their rescue from Egypt, the Israelites spent many years in the desert, partly because they did not believe that God would really give them the Promised Land (Numbers 13). Now, their leader, Joshua, has led the Israelites to the Promised Land once again. God gave the Israelites very specific directions about how to win in the battle against Jericho, but the instructions didn't make much sense! Today, we will learn that **we can always trust God!** (*Open with prayer requests, praises, and a time of prayer.*)

Bible Story

Say: What is the longest walk you have ever taken? (*Children respond.*)

God was going to give the land of Jericho to the Israelites to live in, but they needed to get past a giant wall first. Let's turn in the Bible to Joshua 6. (*Read Joshua 6:2–5.*) I would imagine the Israelites were tired after all that walking! But they trusted God, even when it didn't make much sense to walk around and blow horns, so they obeyed. And God made those walls fall to the ground! Let's read what happened next. (*Read Joshua 6:15–16 and 20.*) The Israelites were able to live in the city of Jericho because they trusted and obeyed God.

Outline
Overview
Bible Story
Opening Game
Object Lesson
Additional Optional Activities

Materials
- Bibles
- Resealable plastic bag
- Water
- Very sharp pencils
- Wooden blocks or cardboard boxes
- Construction paper
- Tape

Opening Game: Follow the Leader

Materials
• None

Say: In today's Bible story, God gave Joshua some very clear instructions about how to knock down the walls of Jericho. We're going to practice following instructions as well, even when it seems silly or doesn't make sense.

Directions: Pick a child to be a leader for two minutes. Leader gives instructions to the rest of the group (either for Simon Says or Follow the Leader). Gently point out when kids do not fully follow instructions, but encourage them to continue in the game. As time allows, other kids take turns to be leader.

DEVELOPMENTAL TIDBITS
What Are They Capable Of?
• Understanding their spiritual gifts
• Being involved in missions
• Learning to share their faith
• Having healthy friendships and boundaries
• Developing a Christian worldview—Critical viewing of media

Turn to page 51 for more Developmental Tidbits.

Object Lesson: Water Bag

Materials

- Resealable plastic bag
- Water
- Very sharp pencils

Preparation: Partially fill plastic bag with water. Seal shut.

Say: I have a plastic bag filled with water and some pencils. Guess what I'm going to do with them? (*Children respond.*)

I'm going to poke these pencils through the plastic bag, but I don't want any water to leak out. If you think I can do it, put your hands on your head. (*Children respond.*)

It doesn't make much sense, does it? Usually when you poke a hole in something that is filled with water, the water leaks out, but today—we're going to try the impossible!

Directions: Hold the bag firmly in your hand by the top and slide the pencils through one side of the plastic bag and out the other side. Don't hesitate or pull the pencil back out!

Say: Amazingly, the bag does not leak! This demonstration didn't make much sense, did it? I bet that's how the Israelites were feeling when they got their instructions for defeating Jericho as well. But we know that we can trust God, even when things don't make much sense. The Israelites obeyed God and walked around the city of Jericho for seven days, just as the Lord commanded, and the walls simply crumbled to the ground. It doesn't make any sense, but it shows us just how powerful God is!

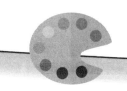

Additional Optional Activities

Build Your Own Wall

Directions: Give kids simple wooden blocks or cardboard boxes and tell them to build a wall (*you may want to set a timer for two or three minutes for this task*). Now, see if the kids can knock over the wall without touching it (*blowing on it, jumping near it, etc*).

Say: It is pretty hard to knock over a wall, even one just made of blocks or boxes. Isn't it amazing that God knocked over the walls of Jericho the way he did? Remind kids that **we can always trust God.**

Blow that Horn

Say: On the final day, the Israelites blew horns just as God commanded. Let's make our own horn to remind us of today's Bible story.

Directions: Using construction paper and tape, have kids wrap a piece of paper around itself to create a horn. Kids decorate it with markers and stickers. If time allows, recreate the horn-blowing part of the story with kids.

Special Music Guest

Say: Today, we have a special guest! We are going to get to hear what a horn might have sounded like when the Israelites were marching around Jericho.

Directions: Invite someone who can play the trumpet to visit the kids during your last few minutes together. Ask them to play a sound or blow their trumpet as loud as they can, reminding us of what happened at Jericho.

Materials
- Wooden blocks or cardboard boxes

Materials
- Construction paper
- Tape

Materials
- None

Chapter 13: Judges

BIBLE STORY REFERENCE: Judges 2:6–19

MEMORY VERSE: *If my people, who are called by my name, will humble themselves and pray and seek my face and turn from their wicked ways, then I will hear from heaven, and I will forgive their sin and will heal their land. 2 Chronicles 7:14*

Big Idea
God Will Forgive Our Sins

Overview

Say: The people had finally made it to the Promised Land! There was plenty of room for everyone and God gave land to each tribe of Israel. However, not all was well in the Promised Land. The Israelites often chose to disobey God and do the wrong thing. (*Open with prayer requests, praises, and a time of prayer.*)

Bible Story

Say: How do we know what is right and what is wrong? (*Children respond.*) It's not always easy to know the right thing to do. God gave us families to help show us right from wrong. He also gave us the Bible which tells us the right thing to do.

The Bible tells us that while their leader Joshua was alive, the Israelites served the one true God. However, once Joshua died, God's people forgot about God and began to disobey him. Let's read about it in Judges 2. (*Read Judges 2:6–19.*)

God directed judges to be leaders for the people and theses judges helped the people turn back to God. But it never lasted long and the people would begin to disobey again. God had to punish them and when they repented, God forgave their sins. **God will forgive our sins,** too. What very good news!

Outline
Overview
Bible Story
Opening Game
Object Lesson
Additional Optional Activities

Materials
- **Bibles**
- **Reproducible page 222**
- **Dry-erase board**
- **Dry-erase markers**
- **Dry-erase eraser**
- **Construction paper**
- **Craft stick**
- **Glue**
- **36-inch dowel**
- **2 black balloons**
- **Black paint**
- **Camera or cell phone**
- **Printer**

Opening Game: Why Are You Famous?

Materials

- None

Say: There were a lot of judges that served Israel. We're going to play a little game to help us get to know some of the judges.

Directions: Play a game of "guess the phrase." Using one of the phrases below, draw blanks on the board to coordinate with the number of letters. Write the alphabet across the top of the board. Have kids guess letters and fill in the letters in the appropriate blanks as they are guessed. Cross off the alphabet as guess letters to make it easier to keep track of what letters are left.

Phrases:

- Samson was super strong.

- Deborah was a brave woman.

- Ehud was left-handed.

- An angel visited Gideon.

- Gideon won a battle with a small army.

- Shamgar fought with an ox goad (farming tool).

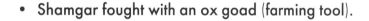

DEVELOPMENTAL TIDBITS
Helpful Learning Tidbits

- Make the environment interactive, stimulating, all tied back to Bible truth
- Use memorizing opportunities—repetition, songs, rhythm, and storytelling
- Support parents by supplying suggestions on home devotion
- Listen for ways the ministry can support and help the family

Turn to page 56 for more Developmental Tidbits.

Object Lesson: Clean Boards

Materials

- Dry-erase board
- Dry-erase markers
- Dry-erase eraser

Say: Has anyone ever done anything bad or sinful? (*Children respond. Write responses on the dry-erase board.*)

Just like all of us, the Israelites did some bad things. They sinned and worshiped fake gods. God does not like sin (Chapter 3: Noah's Ark) and he had to punish the Israelites. God allowed other countries to win battles against the Israelites. When this happened, the Israelites realized their mistakes and repented. They told God they were sorry for what they had done.

What do you think God did when the Israelites repented for their sins? (*Children respond.*) God forgave their sins and **God will forgive our sins**, too. (*As you are saying this, erase the board.*)

Unfortunately, it wasn't too long before the Israelites started sinning again. That's the same for you and me, too. We try our best, but pretty soon, we start doing the same things. (*Rewrite the sins on the dry-erase board.*)

What do you think happens when we do the same things over again? (*Children respond.*) **When we ask, God will forgive our sins.** (*Erase the board.*)

God will always forgive us if we are sorry for what we did, but the trouble is, when we fill up our board with sins, we have no room for good things in our life like kindness, gentleness, and sharing (*Write on the board as you speak.*)

By God's power, we want to keep our boards clean so that we have space in our life to do the good things that God wants us to.

Additional Optional Activities

Ehud, the Left-Handed Judge

Materials
- Reproducible page 222
- Construction paper
- Craft stick
- Glue

Say: Something remarkable about Ehud was the fact that he was left handed. Let's trace our left hands to make a craft that reminds us of Ehud.

Directions: Have kids trace their left hand on one side of construction paper. Have them wrap a craft stick in foil and glue it onto a smaller craft stick to form a sword. Glue the sword onto the left hand that the kids just traced (may need to use tacky glue).

Super Strong Samson

Materials
- 36-inch dowel
- 2 black balloons
- Black paint
- Camera or cell phone
- Printer

Tip: Add some Bible time costumes and a wig to add extra fun to this activity. Kids may want to wear a wig as well since Samson had long hair.

Preparation: Blow up the two black balloons, tie them off. Paint the dowel black. Attach the balloons to the end of the dowel to look like a dumbbell.

Say: Samson was a judge who was known for his incredible strength. Let's lift up this "bar bell" and take a picture to show off your incredible strength.

Directions: Kids children pretending to be super strong. Take pictures of the kids and print them to display around the room.

Fewer and Fewer Soldiers

Materials
- None

Say: Gideon had a very small army. Let's play a game to make our "army" smaller and smaller just like Gideon.

Directions: Play a game like Sharks and Minnows. Kids line up on one side of the room with one child standing in the middle of the room. Kids try to race across the room without getting tagged by the child in the middle. If they are tagged, they sit out for the round. Play until there are only a few children left.

Chapter 14: Ruth

BIBLE STORY REFERENCE: Ruth 1:16–18, 2:8–12, 4:13–32

MEMORY VERSE: *Therefore, as God's chosen people, holy and dearly loved, clothe yourselves with compassion, kindness, humility, gentleness and patience. Colossians 3:12*

Big Idea
God Rewards Kindness

Overview

Say: God wants us to show kindness to one another. (*Read Ephesians 4:32.*) **God rewards kindness** and he rewarded the actions of Ruth. God led her to a field of a man who kept Ruth safe as she gathered in the wheat field. His name was Boaz and he was so impressed with Ruth's kindness and her hard work that he eventually married her. Ruth and Boaz had a baby boy who was the grandfather of King David (Ruth 4:13–17) and an ancestor to Jesus himself. That's a pretty cool reward for her kindness! (*Open with prayer requests, praises, and a time of prayer.*)

Bible Story

Say: Has anyone ever shown kindness to you? How did it make you feel? (*Children respond.*)

Ruth was a girl whose life was filled with kindness. When all the men in her family died and her mother-in-law, Naomi, had no one to help her, Ruth refused to leave Naomi alone. Let's read about it in the book of Ruth. (*Read Ruth 1:16–18.*) She could have stayed in Moab with her own family and found a new husband, but Ruth chose to show kindness to Naomi and **God rewarded her kindness**. God led Ruth to a safe field to gather grain in. (*Read Ruth 2:8–12.*) Eventually Ruth and Boaz married and Naomi helped them raise their baby son.

Outline
Overview
Bible Story
Opening Game
Object Lesson
Additional Optional Activities

Materials
- Bibles
- Small bits of yarn and pipe cleaners
- Bucket
- Water
- Small pebbles
- Paper
- Drawing materials
- Embroidery floss
- Beads

Opening Game: Gleaning in the Field

Materials

- Small bits of yarn and pipe cleaners

Tip: You might want to set a one minute time limit for the first round.

Preparation: Sprinkle small bits of yarn or pipe cleaners on the floor to represent wheat.

Directions: Ask the kids to pretend they are wheat harvesters and to gather up all the grains (yarn). After it is all gathered up, ask one girl to gather up anything that is left. It might take a little searching, but she should be able to find a little something.

Say: This is exactly how Ruth had to find her food. After the workers had gathered up everything, she went through and took what was left. However, you can see it wasn't much.

The Lord provided for Ruth and Naomi, though. He brought Ruth to the field of Boaz and when Boaz saw her, he instructed the workers to leave extra for Ruth. (*Put the yarn back on the ground and instruct the kids to repeat the activity, but this time, they are to leave extra for "Ruth." "Ruth" gathers grain again.*)

Ruth must have been happy to have someone looking out for her. **God rewards kindness** and God rewarded Ruth's kindness by leading her to a field where she would be able to find plenty of wheat.

Object Lesson: Water Ripples

Materials
- Bucket
- Water
- Small pebbles

Bonus Tip: Put some blue dye in water so the ripples are easier to see.

Preparation: Fill bucket with water.

Say: Have you ever gone to a lake or stream and tossed rocks into the water? What happens when the rock hits the water? (*Children respond.*)

Those are all good answers. What we're going to talk about today is ripples. Ripples in the water are a crazy thing. They start out so small and just keep spreading. Let's take a look. (*Drop one pebble in the water and observe the ripples together.*)

You know, these ripples remind me a lot about the kindness Ruth showed to the people in her life. It started out with something small (*Drop a pebble in the water.*), **choosing** to stay with Naomi, and the effects of her kindness kept spreading. **God rewards kindness** and he brought many good things into Ruth's life because of her kindness.

Do you remember some of the good things that happened to Ruth because of her kindness? (*Children respond.*)

God will reward our kindness, too. Let's pray together and ask God to show us someone we can show kindness to this week. (*Close in prayer with the kids, allowing some room for silence if the group is receptive to that.*)

DEVELOPMENTAL TIDBITS

Developmental experts believe the first six years mark a child for life. By age 7, the "personality" mold has been cast. And faith—while still premature—has formed enough to guide future decisions.

Turn to page 60 for more Developmental Tidbits.

Additional Optional Activities

Materials
- Paper
- Drawing materials

Materials
- Embroidery floss
- Beads

Tip: Need some help? Search online for "how to make friendship bracelets."

Link-Up Tag

Say: Ruth refused to leave Naomi's side. She was determined to stick together. In this game, let's stick together as well!

Directions: All kids start in pairs except for two children. One of the unpaired kids will be "It" and the other will be running away from "It." The runner will link up to any pair they see. When they link up to one person in the pair, the other person is now the "runner" and must run away from "It." The runner will again link up to another pair, sending the opposite person running. If it is too easy for "It" to catch the free agent, set three or four kids running to link up to pairs.

I Can Show Kindness

Say: As we saw with Ruth and Naomi, **God rewards kindness**. Let's think of ways we can show kindness in our own community, schools, and homes.

Directions: Have kids draw pictures of ways they can show kindness and display pictures in the room. If one idea especially resonates with the group, try to plan a service project around the idea.

Friendship Bracelets

Say: Ruth and Naomi had an unlikely friendship. It was pretty neat that they cared and looked out for each other. They were very kind. Let's make friendship bracelets to remind us that **God rewards kindness**.

Directions: Make bracelets with kids with beads or embroidery floss. Encourage them to give one to a friend at school or a sibling. You may want to practice ahead of time and have a few samples ready for the kids to look at.

Chapter 15: Samuel

BIBLE STORY REFERENCE: 1 Samuel 3:1–18

MEMORY VERSE: *Samuel said, "Speak, for your servant is listening."* 1 Samuel 3:10

Big Idea
I Can Listen to God

Overview

Say: Samuel was a special child. His mother, Hannah, could not have children for many years. She prayed to God in desperation one year at the temple, asking God for a baby. She promised that she would allow the child to live in the temple and serve the Lord all his life if God would grant her request. God did indeed give Hannah a baby boy and she took Samuel to the temple so that he could serve God with the priest, Eli. It was a big responsibility for a little boy, and as he grew, Samuel took his job very seriously. (*Open with prayer requests, praises, and a time of prayer.*)

Bible Story

 Say: When you want to talk to someone, what do you usually do? (*Children respond.*)

When we want to talk with God, we pray to him. We can tell God anything and he loves to hear from us. We can listen to God too. Usually, God talks to us by giving us a special feeling in our hearts or a quiet thought in our minds. Sometimes God uses a parent to tell us something we need to hear. It's not often that people hear an actual voice from God, but Samuel did, when he was just a boy living in the temple. Let's read about it in **1 Samuel 3.** (*Read 1 Samuel 3:1–18.*) What an amazing experience for Samuel. We might not hear God like Samuel did, but **we can listen to God.**

Outline
Overview
Bible Story
Opening Game
Object Lesson
Additional Optional Activities

Materials
• Bibles
• Reproducible page 223
• Phone
• Letter from a friend
• Scissors
• Audio Bible story or phone application

Opening Game: Telephone

Say: At first, Samuel didn't realize the Lord was talking to him. When he did listen to God, God's message was very clear. In our game today, though, I think things are going to get a little jumbled!

Directions: Kids sit in a circle or around a table. Pick a phrase (might want to keep it short for the first round). It can be something totally silly or related to the lesson. Whisper the sentence to the child next to you. Then, they whisper it to the child next to them. It goes all around the circle until the final child says it out loud. It usually gets pretty mixed up by the end of the circle! To make it even more difficult, make sure each child only whispers it once to the person next to them. No repeats!

Here are a few phrases to get you started:

- The cow jumped over the moon.

- I like to eat peanut butter and jelly sandwiches.

- Last night, I saw two turtles in my garden.

- We can listen to God.

- I love to read the Bible.

- Today is the day that the Lord has made.

- Be kind to one another.

Object Lesson: Listening to God

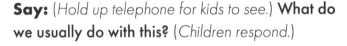

Materials

- Telephone
- Letter from a friend

Say: (*Hold up telephone for kids to see.*) **What do we usually do with this?** (*Children respond.*)

Those are all good answers. We use the phone to communicate with others. We can call them. We can send them a picture. We can send them a text message. These are all ways we can talk with others with a phone. (*Hold up the letter for kids to see.*)

What about this? What do you think this is? (*Children respond.*)

That's right—this is a letter from a friend. Before there were phones, people used to write letters to each other to communicate. But to send a letter, you need a stamp and a post office, and it takes awhile for it to get to someone.

Nowadays, we can use a cell phone almost any place, but there are places that it won't work. But do you know one method of communication that always works, no matter where you are or what time of day it is? Prayer.

We can talk to God anytime and anywhere. He is always listening to us. **We can listen to God,** too. Our message from God might not be as clear as Samuel's, but God has other ways of talking with us. It can be through his letter to us, the Bible. Or sometimes it's a feeling in our hearts—the Holy Spirit tells us to be kind to someone or to obey our parents, even when we don't really feel like it. The more we get to know God, the easier it is to listen to him.

DEVELOPMENTAL TIDBITS

If their faith has been productively and positively developed, by age 10, children will make pronounced and powerful individualized faith commitments.

Turn to page 63 for more Developmental Tidbits.

Materials

- Reproducible page 223
- Scissors

Materials

- Audio Bible story or phone application

Bonus Idea: Break the children into groups and have them invent signs of their own to the verse. Have each of them show the class their idea.

Charades

Preparation: Copy, cut out, and use the cards on page 223.

Say: In our Bible story, Samuel heard the voice of God, but in this game, no talking is allowed!

Directions: One child picks a card and acts it out using no words and the other kids try to guess.

Listen to the Story

Say: Samuel did some listening in today's Bible story. Let's do some listening of our own as we listen to the day's Bible story.

Directions: Sometimes, listening to the Bible story really helps it come to life for some kids. Especially on a day when the Bible story is about listening! Using a dramatized audio Bible (there are many apps for this), play the day's Bible story (1 Samuel 3) for the kids.

Sign Language

Say: Let's learn some sign language for our verse today so we can share it with others without even talking.

Directions: Use an online resource to learn the American Sign Language motions for the words of the verse. Teach kids the sign language. If time allows, video the kids as a group and show the video next week as a form of review.

dirty

rain

hug

Chapter 16: David as Shepherd

BIBLE STORY REFERENCE: Psalms 23

MEMORY VERSE: *The Lord is my shepherd, I lack nothing.* Psalm 23:1

Big Idea
God Wants Us to Spend Time with Him

Overview

Say: When David was a boy, he helped the family by keeping watch over the sheep. He was a shepherd. The sheep usually didn't wander far and while David was watching them, he had some extra time on his hands. Instead of watching TV (there was no such thing!), David spent his time talking to God and writing songs about him. We can find many of these songs in the book of Psalms. (*Open with prayer requests, praises, and a time of prayer.*)

Bible Story

Say: Have you ever written a poem? What was it about? (*Children respond.*)

David spent a lot of time writing poems while he was a shepherd. David liked to turn his poems into songs and sing them to the Lord. One poem many people enjoy is Psalm 23. Let's read it together. (*Read Psalm 23.*) David also spent a lot of time praying to God. We can read many of these prayers in the Psalms as well. **God wants us to spend time with him,** both through praying and reading the Bible. It helps us get to know God and it helps us know the right thing to do.

Outline
Overview
Bible Story
Opening Game
Object Lesson
Additional Optional Activities

Materials
- **Bibles**
- **Reproducible page 224**
  - **Cotton balls**
  - **Hymn book**
- **Dry-erase board**
- **Dry-erase marker**
- **Dry-erase eraser**
  - **Clothespin**
- **Construction paper**
  - **Wiggly eyes**
  - **Straw**
  - **Glue**
- **Pencils or markers**
  - **Poster board**

Opening Game: Little Lost Sheep

Materials
- Cotton balls

Preparation: Get a bag of cotton balls and hide them throughout the room. Make sure there are at least three to five cotton balls for each child to find.

Say: David's job was to keep the family's sheep safe. Sometimes sheep wander off and get stuck in thorn bushes where a lion or bear could easily eat them or they fall into a river where their wet, heavy wool would make it too hard to get out. In this game, there are cotton-ball sheep lost all over the room. There should be enough for each of you to find at least three. When you have found at least three lost sheep, bring them back to the table (or your gathering space).

BEHAVIOR MANAGEMENT TIDBITS
Dangerous or Inappropriate Behaviors
(Like self-injury, hitting others, throwing objects, etc.)

- Be firm and structured
- Provide clear instructions and be as specific as possible (ex: listen, hands down, come here, sit down, quiet hands, quiet voice)
- Clearly and concisely state in firm voice with no emotions
- Do not threaten or repeat instruction more than once or twice.

Turn to page 67 for more Behavior Management Tidbits.

Object Lesson: Songs, Psalms & Hymns

Materials

- Hymn book
- Dry-erase board
- Dry-erase marker
- Dry-erase eraser

Say: Does anyone have a favorite hymn or a song we sing in church? (*Children respond. Write responses on the dry-erase board.*)

Just like David wrote songs, many other people throughout years wrote songs. Tell the kids one of your favorite hymns, showing it to them in the hymn book. If possible, give a brief background on the composer or song itself. **God wants us to spend time with him** thinking about the good things he has done, and thanking him for it is one way we can do that.

(*Hold up the hymn book. Flip through the pages.*) This book is full of songs that tell about God's power, God's forgiveness, God's healing, and more. The people who wrote these hymns probably spent a lot of time with God and wanted to show God how much they loved him by writing a song. The wonderful thing is, these songs help other people to draw closer to God, too.

When can it be hard to spend time with God? (*Children respond.*)

Directions: If time permits, brainstorm together ways you can overcome obstacles to spending time with God.

Say: God wants us to spend time with him and the amazing thing is, the more we get to know God, the more we want to spend time with him. Let's ask God to help us as we strive to spend more time with him this week. (*Close activity in prayer.*)

Materials

- Cotton balls
- Clothespin
- Construction paper
- Wiggly eyes
- Straw
- Glue

Tip: You may need to hot glue the cotton balls on for the kids.

Materials

- Reproducible page 224
- Pencils or markers
- Poster board

Materials

- None

Shepherd and His Sheep

Say: Let's make a craft to remind us of the shepherd we read about in Psalm 23.

Directions: Using the cotton balls from the game earlier, create this adorable 3-D craft with the kids. For the shepherd, use a clothespin (you may need to hot glue it in place for the kids), drawing a face on a little scrap of construction paper if you like. Glue eyes onto the cotton balls and add a cutoff straw for the staff (glue directly to the shepherd).

Write Your Own Poems and Songs

Preparation: Copy the page 224, making one for each child.

Say: David spent a lot of time writing songs and poems. Let's try our hand at writing our own!

Directions: Children fill in the blanks. Brainstorm ideas as a group. Children may also form groups to write songs. After group is happy with their songs, they copy songs onto poster board with markers to display in the room.

Have You Seen My Sheep?

Directions: Children stand or sit in a circle. Select a player to be the "Shepherd" and stand outside the circle. "Shepherd" taps someone's back and says, "Have you seen my sheep?"

The tapped player is now the "Housekeeper," and asks "What does he look like?"

"Shepherd" then describes a seated child, saying something like "He has black shoes, a red shirt, and brown hair." The described child, the "Lost Sheep," gets up and starts to run around the circle. "Housekeeper" tries to tag "Lost Sheep" before player can run. Otherwise, "Housekeeper" chases "Lost Sheep" around the circle. "Lost Sheep" tries to return to his spot before being caught by "Housekeeper."

Chapter 17: David as King

BIBLE STORY REFERENCE: Psalm 119:10–11, 47–48;
1 Samuel 16:7

MEMORY VERSE: *People look at the outward appearance,
but the Lord looks at the heart. 1 Samuel 16:7*

Big Idea
God Looks at the Heart

Overview

Say: David spent a long time as a shepherd before he was a king. While he was a shepherd, David spent his time talking to God and writing songs about him. David grew to love God and he wanted to obey his commands. When Samuel came to David's family to anoint a new king, he was surprised that God did not pick one of the tall, strong, older brothers. **God looks at the heart** and God wanted a king who would obey him. We can see by David's actions and David's words (in the Psalms) that he loved God and honored him. God wants us to love him with our hearts as well. (*Open with prayer requests, praises, and a time of prayer.*)

Bible Story

 Say: What do you think it means when God looks at the heart? (*Children respond.*)

When God looks at the heart, he sees the things we love the most. David loved God with his heart and that is what made him such a good king. David tried to obey God's commands and do the right thing. Let's turn in the Bible to Psalm 119:10–11 and 47–48. (*Read Scripture aloud.*) When Samuel was picking out a new king, God told him not to look at height, strength, or good looks. Let's read 1 Samuel 16:7. (*Read Scripture aloud.*) **God looks at the heart** because that is the most important thing.

Outline
Overview
Bible Story
Opening Game
Object Lesson
Additional Optional Activities

Materials
- **Bibles**
- **Everyday objects**
  - **Boxes**
  - **Paper**
  - **Pencil**
- **X-ray or ultrasound image**
  - **Bible**
- **Black construction paper**
  - **White paint**
  - **Paint brushes**
  - **Heart stickers**
- **Foam heart cut-out**
- **Washable markers**
  - **Sink or basin of water and soap**
  - **Children's verse songs and players**
  - **Headphones**
- **Pillows or cushions**

Opening Game: What's Inside?

Materials
- Everyday objects (suggestions below)
- Boxes with lids, one for each object
- Tape
- Paper
- Pencil

Box content suggestions:
Teddy bear, paper clips, tissues, coins, Legos or blocks, pair of shoes, wash cloth, pair of socks, ball, crayons, pens, small board books, hair brush, and silverware

Preparation: Put everyday objects inside boxes, place lids on top, and tape secure. Number the boxes on the outside.

Directions: Ask a volunteer (one for each box) to shake the box as the rest of the group listens. Allow kids to guess what is inside and write down answers, using the box numbers to keep track of each one. When all the boxes have been shaken and guesses have been made, open up the boxes to reveal what is inside.

Say: We took some guesses about what was inside these boxes, but we didn't know for sure. Did you know that God knows everything? He knew what was inside these boxes and he knows what is inside of us. He knows what we are thinking and feeling all the time. **God looks at the heart** and he wants us to love us with everything we have inside.

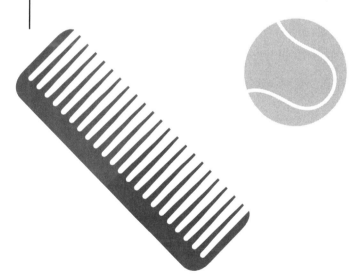

BEHAVIOR MANAGEMENT TIDBITS
Dangerous or Inappropriate Behaviors
- Immediately reinforce or praise as soon as you see any de-escalation in behavior.
- Firmly communicate what to do, not what NOT to do.
- Provide options (sit down, quiet hands, let's go for a walk).
- Be specific as possible what needs to be done with a firm and unemotional voice.
- Lastly, separate the child from other children and contact leadership and child's parents.

Turn to page 72 for more Behavior Management Tidbits.

Object Lesson: Seeing the Heart

Materials

- X-ray or ultrasound image

Tip: You can print one off the internet, or bring in a book on the body from your local library.

Say: What is this a picture of? (*Children respond.*) It's pretty crazy that we can see inside a person's body like this!

Doctors can use X-ray machines and sonogram machines to see inside a person to make sure everything is okay. In our Bible story today, Samuel the prophet was in charge of picking a new king for God's special people, the Israelites. Samuel wasn't exactly sure what to look for, but God told him to go to the house of Jesse. (*Read 1 Samuel 16:5–13.*)

When Samuel saw the oldest son, Eliab, he was impressed. He must have looked like a movie star or a great athlete. But God was not interested in what Eliab looked like on the outside. God was interested in what was inside.

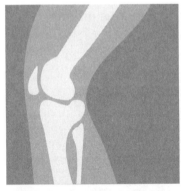
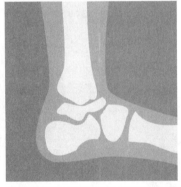
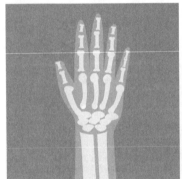
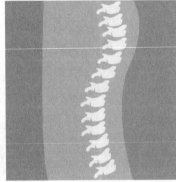

God wanted a king who would be kind to others, who would do the right thing, and who would obey God's commands. God could tell that Eliab's heart was not right—and he could do it without any special medical equipment! God chose David to be king because David loved God. God looks at the heart and he wants us to love him, too.

(*Read Psalm 139:23–24.*) Pray aloud, asking God to reveal any sin that might be in our lives. Ask **God to look at our hearts** and help us to love him more.

Additional Optional Activities

Materials

- Black construction paper
- White paint
- Paint brushes
- Heart stickers

Materials

- Foam heart cut-out
- Washable markers
- Sink or basin of water and soap

Materials

- Children's verse songs and players
- Headphones
- Pillows or cushions

Tip: To find verse songs to use, do an online search for "Children's verse songs."

God Looks At the Heart

Say: When the Bible says, **"God looks at the heart,"** it means that God cares about the character of a person. In this craft though, we'll be taking a more literal approach.

Directions: Using white paint and black construction paper, kids paint a rib cage. In the center of the rib cage, put a heart sticker. Children write "1 Samuel 16:7" on the paper.

Create in Me a Clean Heart

Directions: Kids use washable markers to write sins on a foam hearts. Then, they wash their hearts clean in a basin of soapy water.

Say: King David wanted to make sure he was doing the right thing. When he disobeyed God, he asked for forgiveness. God promises to forgive our sins and make our hearts clean again when we ask him to.

Listening Station

Say: King David continued to write Psalms and songs when he was a king. Let's spend some time listening to songs written from verses in the Bible.

Directions: Kids listen to verse songs. Set up a station in the room with a variety of children's verse songs, players, and headphones. Use pillows and cushions to make it comfortable.

Chapter 18: King Solomon

BIBLE STORY REFERENCE: 2 Chronicles 1:7–12; 1 King 10:1–9

MEMORY VERSE: *Give me wisdom and knowledge, that I may lead this people. 2 Chronicles 1:10*

Big Idea
God Gives Us Wisdom

Overview

Say: After David was king, his son Solomon became king over all of God's people. God spoke to Solomon one night and offered him any request. (*Read 2 Chronicles 1:7–13.*) Instead of wealth or a long life, Solomon asked for wisdom and God was very pleased. **God gives us wisdom** too, if we ask him for it. (*Open with prayer requests, praises, and a time of prayer.*)

Bible Story

Say: What might we need wisdom for? (*Children respond.*)

Sometimes we need to make hard choices when we are at school or at home. It's not always easy to know the right thing to do. God gives us wisdom and he will help us make the right choice.

The Bible is full of God's wisdom. The more we read the Bible, the more wisdom we will gain from God. We can also gain wisdom from older Christians such as parents, grandparents, and teachers. Let's read James 1:5 from the Bible. (*Read Scripture aloud.*)

King Solomon asked God for wisdom when he became king. Let's read 2 Chronicles 1:7–12. (*Read Scripture aloud.*) Solomon's wisdom was so great people came from all over to ask him questions and get his advice. Even a great queen traveled from far away to see Solomon and hear his wisdom (*1 King 10:1–9*).

Outline
Overview
Bible Story
Opening Game
Object Lesson
Additional Optional Activities

Materials
- Bibles
- Reproducible page 225
  - Owl puppet
  - Cardstock
  - Craft stick
  - Scissors
  - Markers
- Various spices
- Blindfold
- Treasure chest picture
- Toy gold coins

Opening Game: Who Could It Be?

Materials

- None

Say: Let's play a guessing game and see if you can remember the people we've learned about!

Directions: Give clues (see examples below) and then ask, "Who could it be?" Kids guess out loud, playing as time and interest allow.

- This person lost many things they cared about, but they still trusted God. (Job)

- This person built a giant boat to save his family and the animals of the world. (Noah)

- These people were the first humans on Earth. (Adam and Eve)

- These people helped turn God's people back towards God after they sinned and worshiped fake gods. (The judges)

- This man traded his birthright for a bowl of stew. (Esau)

- This person was sold to traveling merchants by his own brothers. (Joseph)

- Satan disguised himself as this and tricked Adam and Eve into eating forbidden fruit. (Snake or serpent)

- These people had to wait a very long time for their promised baby son. (Abraham and Sarah)

- This man led the people in a great battle around a city named Jericho. (Joshua)

- This man had twelve sons and loved one son more than the others. (Jacob)

- This man was rescued from the Nile River and raised in the palace as a prince. (Moses)

- This woman stayed with her mother-in-law and showed her kindness. (Ruth)

- This man confronted Pharaoh and demanded that Pharaoh let God's people go. (Moses)

- This person spent a long time as a shepherd before he became king. (David)

Object Lesson: Wise Like an Owl

Materials
• Owl puppet

Say: *(Hold up the owl puppet.)* **What kind of animal is this? What is this animal usually known for?** *(Children respond.)*

Owls are often associated with wisdom. It may be because they are usually quiet and still, watching and observing what is happening around them.

Watching and waiting is a good way to show wisdom. Sometimes we react quickly when we are upset instead of calming ourselves down and acting with wisdom.

(Use the owl puppet.) **Whooooo gives wisdom?** *(Children respond.)* **God gives us wisdom**!

• God can give us wisdom when we are studying for a test.

• God can give us wisdom when we are trying to decide what activities to participate in.

• God can give us wisdom when we are talking to a friend about Jesus.

God gives us wisdom about all kinds of things. God knows all things and he is the best source of wisdom there is!

BEHAVIOR MANAGEMENT TIDBITS
Encouraging Appropriate Behaviors

• Praise in public
• Aim internal rewards not external
• Developing self-discipline and personal responsibility
• Discipline in private
• Create simple and consistent rules
• Keep in mind you are modeling God, forgiveness, unconditional love
• Remember they crave approval and connection.

Turn to page 75 for more Behavior Management Tidbits.

Additional Optional Activities

Materials
- Reproducible page 225
- Cardstock
- Craft stick
- Scissors
- Markers

Bonus Idea: Provide craft supplies like beads, feathers, sequins, etc. to decorate masks.

Materials
- Various spices
- Blindfold

Materials
- Treasure chest picture
- Toy gold coins, available at party stores

Owl Mask

Directions: For each child copy the owl mask onto cardstock. Kids cut out and color masks. Cut out eyes so kids can see through the mask. Attach a craft stick to the bottom. Often, you can find wooden stick puppets at craft stores.

Say: Use the mask to retell the story to your friends and family. Let them know that God is whoooo we should go to for wisdom.

The Queen's Spices

Say: The Queen of Sheba brought many gifts to Solomon. Among the gifts were a variety of exotic spices as a gift. Let's check out some spices and play a smelling game.

Directions: Blindfold a volunteer (or have them close their eyes) and have them smell a spice and guess what it is. If they guess wrong, take off the blindfold and have them guess again. If they guess wrong a second time, pour a small amount into their hand to taste. If volunteer still guesses wrong, ask other kids to guess. Continue with different volunteers and different spices.

Wisdom Is Better Than Gold

Say: When God granted Solomon any wish, Solomon chose wisdom instead of gold or power. God was very pleased with Solomon's choice. Let's make a craft that reminds us that God gives us wisdom.

Directions: Draw a simple treasure chest on a piece of white paper. Make copies for all the kids. Have kids glue toy gold coins around the treasure chest. Under the chest, write "Wisdom is better than gold" along with the reference 2 Chronicles 7:12.

Chapter 19: Josiah

BIBLE STORY REFERENCE: 2 Kings 22:1–20

MEMORY VERSE: *When the king heard the words of the Book of the Law, he tore his robes. 2 Kings 22:11*

Big Idea
Good Kings Obey God

Overview

Say: After Solomon was king, Israel had a big fight and the kingdom was divided into two parts: Israel and Judah. After the kingdom was divided, there were many kings who ruled over Israel and Judah. Some kings loved and obeyed God, and some kings did not. **Good kings obey God**. God blessed the kings who obeyed him and who chose to do the right thing. Josiah was a king who obeyed God. He was only a boy when he became king (2 Kings 22:1). He obeyed God during his reign and even had God's temple rebuilt. (*Open with prayer requests, praises, and a time of prayer.*)

Bible Story

Say: King Josiah ruled over the land of Judah. One day, as the temple was being repaired, an interesting discovery was made! Let's turn to 2 Kings 22:8–10 in the Bible. (*Read Scripture aloud.*) King Josiah was surprised to find the law of the Lord lost in the temple. He was also upset that the people had not been keeping the law. He immediately told the people to begin doing the right thing because **good kings obey God**. Because Josiah responded right away to the law of the Lord, he would not see disaster during his reign as king. Let's read 2 Kings 22:18–20. (*Read Scripture aloud.*) Good kings obey God and we should obey God, too!

Outline
Overview
Bible Story
Opening Game
Object Lesson
Additional Optional Activities

Materials
- Bibles
- Cardboard boxes
- Large markers
- Smoke alarm
- Very small dowel rods
- Tan construction paper
- Glue or tape
- Twine
- Hebrew letter chart
- Cleaning supplies
- Toy building supplies

Opening Game: Destroy the Idols

Materials

- Cardboard boxes
- Large markers

Preparation: On one side of the room, stack boxes two or three boxes high. Make one box stack for each team of three or four players. Draw a stick-figure fake idol on each stack of boxes.

Say: Josiah loved God and worshiped him only. **Good kings obey God.** Other kings who ruled over Judah and Israel worshiped fake gods, called idols. In this game, we are going to destroy the idols to show we only want to worship the one true God.

Directions: Children form teams of three or four players and line up opposite the "fake idols." One your signal, the first player on each team will race towards their team's idol, punch or kick idol over and run back to tag the next person in line. The next player runs to the boxes, restacks them, aligning the stick figure correctly and then returns to the team. The third player knocks the idol over again and returns to team. Play continues until every team member has a turn.

BEHAVIOR MANAGEMENT TIDBITS

Consider: What factors are playing out in the life of a challenging child that may be contributing to their behavior. Just some of the conditions that could be factoring into their behavior—family issues, peer pressure, traumatic experiences, cultural confusion, awareness of weakness, special needs, world events, self-image.

Turn to page 83 for tidbits on Learning Styles.

Object Lesson: Action Required!

Materials

- Smoke alarm

Say: Does anyone know what this is and what it does? (*Children respond.*) **This is a smoke detector (or smoke alarm), and it helps keep us safe. Whenever you hear this beeping, it means there is smoke nearby.**

What are you supposed to do if you hear the smoke alarm? (*Children respond.*) **Hopefully your family has talked about a safe way to get out of the house and a place to meet in case there is a fire. But the important thing is to get out!**

Imagine a smoke alarm goes off while you're playing a video game. Do you think it would be okay to finish your game? (*Children respond.*) **Do you think it would be okay to pack a few snacks?** (*Children respond.*)

I hope you all said no! You have to act right away. In our Bible story today, there was a king who got some news. Let's read about it. (*Read 2 Kings 22:8, 10–11, 16–20.*) **King Josiah found a book when he was repairing the temple. When he read it, he realized that the people were not keeping God's rules.**

King Josiah did not wait to act! He repented right away and asked God what he could do in this situation. God was glad that Josiah acted right away and said that he would show mercy because Josiah took immediate action. When we realize we are doing something wrong, we should act right away as well. Just like good kings obey God, we should start doing the right thing as soon as we can.

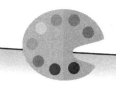

Additional Optional Activities

Materials

- Very small dowel rods, two for each child
- Tan construction paper
- Glue or tape
- Twine
- Hebrew letter chart, available online

Bonus Idea: Before class, use an online translation tool to translate each child's name to Hebrew.

Make Your Own Hebrew Scrolls

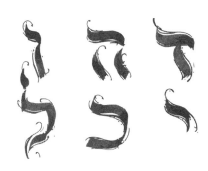

Directions: Using two dowel rods and a piece of tan paper, help the kids make their own scroll. Glue or tape the dowel rods to the ends of the papers (lengthwise). Roll the paper inward and secure with twine. If time allows, have kids try writing some Hebrew letters in their scroll. If Hebrew seems too difficult, have them write a favorite memory verse in English instead.

Say: King Josiah obeyed what was written in the scroll right away because **good kings obey God.**

Materials

- Cleaning supplies (disposable wipes, rags, brooms, feather dusters, window cleaner, etc.)

Bonus Idea: Arrange for a toy cleaning day for the younger classes. Have families come in and clean all the toys in the nursery and preschool rooms. Set up tubs of soapy water and provide snacks.

Cleaning Up God's House

Say: King Josiah did not like to see God's house in disrepair. He hired men to fix God's temple and make it beautiful once again. We can help take care of God's house as well.

Directions: Give kids cleaning supplies such as disposable wipes, dusting rags, and window cleaner (older kids) and have them clean around the church.

Materials

- Toy building supplies

Building a Temple

Say: It was important to keep God's house standing strong. King Josiah hired men to make repairs where needed. Let's build our own temple to God.

Directions: Supply the kids with different building supplies such as wooden blocks, Lincoln Logs, and Legos so they can construct and "repair" their own temples to the Lord.

Chapter 20: Elijah

MEMORY VERSE: *This is what the Lord, the God of Israel, says: "The jar of flour will not be used up and the jug of oil will not run dry until the day the Lord sends rain on the land." 1 Kings 17:14*

Big Idea
God Provides For Us

Overview

Say: Elijah was a prophet of the Lord. Prophets give messages to people from God. During his lifetime, Elijah gave messages to kings—including the very mean and wicked King Ahab. He also had a challenge with the prophets of a fake god (1 Kings 18), and helped many people. When it was time for Elijah to die, God came and picked him up in a chariot of fire (2 Kings 2). When Elijah was on Earth serving God, God provided food and water for him. God provided for Elijah and **God provides for us,** too. (*Open with prayer requests, praises, and a time of prayer.*)

Bible Story

Say: What is something that God has provided in your life? (*Children respond.*)

God provides for us in many different ways. He gives us food to eat and people that care about us. God often helps us to feel better when we are sick and helps us to make good choices when we are at school. God provided for Elijah as well. When Elijah was in the wilderness with no food or water, he met a widow. He asked the widow for food and she told him she had very little. However, God did something amazing! Let's read about it in 1 Kings 17:13–16. God provided for Elijah and the widow by making sure her flour and oil did not run out. Everyone was able to eat for a long time because **God provided for them.**

Outline
Overview
Bible Story
Opening Game
Object Lesson
Additional Optional Activities

Materials
- **Bibles**
- **Reproducible page 226**
- **Reproducible page 227**
- **Loaf of crusty bread**
  - **Mixing bowl**
    - **Spoon**
    - **Flour**
    - **Oil**
- **Cooking magazines**
  - **Paper plates**
  - **Scissors**
- **Bread ingredients**
  - **Mixing bowl**
  - **Spoon**
- **Disposable wipes**
  - **Cotton swabs**
- **Orange, red, and yellow paint**
  - **Small plates**
  - **Cardstock**

Opening Game: Elijah Relay Race

Materials

- Reproducible page 226

Preparation: Copy the reproducible page making at least one picture for each child. Assign point values to each picture (see chart below for help), keeping the chart a surprise until the end of the race. Cut the pictures out individually and put them face down on the floor at the end of the race or on the wall, with the pictures hidden.

Say: In this game, you will race to a wall to pick a picture and return to your team. Each picture has a secret point value, so try to get as many points for your as you can!

Directions: When the race begins, kids will run to the end of the course, grab a picture and return to their team, relay race style. When everyone on the teams have had a chance to run, gather up the pictures and add them up. Whichever team has the most points, based on the Elijah chart, repeats the memory verse or tells a sentence about the Bible story.

PICTURE	POINT VALUE
RAVEN	+5
WIDOW'S SICK SON	+10
BREAD	+5
FIRE FROM HEAVEN	+15
WATER JUG	+10
KING'S CROWN	-10

Object Lesson: Mixing Up Some Bread

Materials

- Loaf of crusty bread (Italian loaf or similar)
- Mixing bowl
- Spoon
- Flour
- Oil

Bonus Idea: Copy the recipe below and send home with each child to try with their family.

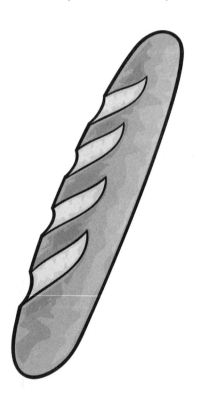

Say: Does anyone here like bread? (*Children respond.*)

In the Bible, bread was often eaten by people. In our Bible story, Elijah asked a widow to make him some bread out of flour and olive oil (*Pour flour and olive oil into the bowl.*). **The woman was worried that she would not have enough food for herself and her son, but Elijah told her that God would provide.** (*Read 1 Kings 17:13–14. Use spoon to mix ingredients in bowl.*)

God provided for this family and God provides for us, too. The bread was not fancy (*Continue mixing.*), but it was what they needed to survive.

God does not always give us the things we want. We don't always get fancy things, but **God provides for us** in his perfect ways.

Directions: Explain that the bread Elijah and the widow had was made of simple flour and oil, similar to your mixture. However, you brought some prebaked bread for samples. Cut the bread into small portions and pass out to the kids to enjoy as a snack.

Unleavened Bread Recipe

2 cups of flour

1 teaspoon of salt

1 tablespoon of olive oil

½ cup of warm water

In a large bowl, combine flour and salt. Stir in olive oil with a fork. Gradually add water until you have a nice soft dough. Add more than ½ cup water if needed.

Pinch off pieces of dough and either roll or pat them into a circle. Poke the breads with a fork. You can then drizzle with additional oil if you like. Bake at 375°F for three to five minutes.

Materials

- Cooking magazines
- Paper plates
- Scissors

Alternate Idea: In addition to magazines, provide old cookbooks or clip art of food. You could also have kids draw pictures of their favorite food on the plate.

Materials

- Bread ingredients, page 80
- Mixing bowl
- Spoon
- Disposable wipes

Materials

- Reproducible page 227
- Cotton swabs
- Orange, red, and yellow paint
- Small plates
- Cardstock

God Provides Food

Say: Let's look through these magazines and make a plate of "food," remembering that God provides for us.

Directions: Give each child a paper plate. Children look through magazines and cut out their favorite foods or foods that **God provides for us**. It might be a good idea to provide a snack during this time so kids don't get hungry looking at all the food!

Make Your Own Bread

Say: God provided for Elijah and he will provide for us, too. Let's make some simple bread to remind us of the bread Elijah ate with the widow.

Directions: Set up a station for kids to recreate the bread made during the lesson. Since it's such a simple recipe, many kids can mix it up on their own. Be sure to provide disposable wipes or a hand washing station for before and after cooking. If you do not have access to an oven, the bread can be eaten safely without cooking.

Fire From Heaven

Say: One of the biggest moments in Elijah's life was the challenge on Mount Carmel (1 Kings 18). Elijah wanted the people to see who the one true God was. God provided for Elijah by sending fire from heaven to burn up the offering. Let's make a craft to remind us of our Bible story.

Directions: Instruct kids to dip cotton swab in orange, red, and yellow paint. Use these colors to paint fire from heaven, using the reproducible page provided.

Chapter 21: Elisha

BIBLE STORY REFERENCE: 2 Kings 5: 9–14

MEMORY VERSE: *I know that there is no God in all the world except in Israel. 2 Kings 5:15*

Big Idea
We Can Help Others

Overview

Say: Elisha was a prophet like Elijah. He gave messages to people from God. He helped people and healed people through God's power. He was very famous in the land of Israel. One day, when a man named Naaman became very sick, Naaman's servant girl knew just what to do. She told her master about Elisha, a man of God who could help Naaman. (*Open with prayer requests, praises, and a time of prayer.*)

Bible Story

Say: In our Bible story today, something sad happened to a little girl. There was a battle in her land, and she was taken away from her family. She was forced to become a servant in a new house. Even though she might have been sad or mad, when her master became sick, she was still willing to help him. **We can help others,** too, even when it is hard. This servant girl told her master, Naaman, about God's prophet Elisha. Let's read about it in 2 Kings 5:9–14. (*Read Scripture aloud.*) **Because** the servant girl was willing to help others, Naaman was healed.

Outline
Overview
Bible Story
Opening Game
Object Lesson
Additional Optional Activities

Materials
- **Bibles**
- **Number cubes**
- **Paper**
- **Marker**
- **Newspaper**
- **Large envelope**
- **Marker**
- **Home-decor magazines**
- **Scissors**
- **Glue**
- **Construction paper**
- **Video camera or cell phone**
- **Newscast props**
- **Washable markers**
- **Basin of soapy water**

Opening Game: Seven Times

Materials

- Number cube, one for each pair of children
- Paper
- Marker

Say: In today's Bible story, Elisha gave Naaman some pretty strange instructions in order to be healed. Naaman was surprised—and a little mad—about the instructions Elisha gave him, but he obeyed anyway. In this game, we'll be thinking about the number seven as we race to cross off each number.

Directions: Give each pair of kids a piece of paper and a number cube. Have each child write the numbers 1–6 on a sheet of paper. Kids take turns rolling a number cube. Whatever number the cube lands on is the number they cross out on the paper. The first person to cross off all the numbers on their paper tells, or chooses a volunteer to tell, a sentence about the Bible story.

LEARNING TIDBITS
Learning Styles

LEARNING STYLES		SENSES
VISUAL	⟷	SEEING
AUDITORY	⟷	HEARING
TACTILE	⟷	TOUCHING
KINESTHETIC	⟷	DOING, TASTING, SMELLING

Turn to page 84 for more Learning Tidbits.

Object Lesson: Good News

Materials

- Newspaper
- Large envelope
- Marker

Preparation: Print "Good News" on the front of the large envelope. Inside the envelope place something from the newspaper that would be good news to the kids (Fun event coming to town, etc.)

Say: This is a newspaper and it tells us the latest news. Some of the stuff is good news and some of the stuff is bad news. Of course, I kind of like the good news best. In fact, I liked one thing so much that I cut it out of the paper and stuck it inside this envelope. (*Hold up "Good News" envelope for the kids to see.*)

How would you feel if I kept this good news to myself and didn't tell you what was in it? (*Children respond.*)

There was a girl in our Bible story today that knew about the one true God. She knew that God could heal her master, Naaman. She could have kept this good news to herself, but she didn't! She chose to share the good news with Naaman's wife. She chose to help others.

We can help others, too. We can tell them about the one true God or we can help them with talents that we have. We shouldn't keep good things to ourselves. We can use them to help others instead.

What are some ways we can help others with the things that we know or the things we can do?

Directions: After kids are done discussing, reveal the "Good News" hidden inside the envelope.

LEARNING TIDBIT

Developmental experts believe the first six years mark a child for life. By age 7, the "personality" mold has been cast. And faith—while still premature—has formed enough to guide future decisions.

Turn to page 87 for more Learning Tidbits.

Additional Optional Activities

Materials
- Home-decor magazines
- Scissors
- Glue
- Construction paper

Materials
- Video camera or cell phone
- Newscast props

Optional
- Toy microphone
- Sheets of paper

Bonus Idea: Create a backdrop.

Materials
- Washable markers
- Basin of soapy water

A Room for You

Directions: Using furniture catalogs have the kids cut out a bed and some other trappings for a room for Elisha. Have them design a space for Elisha like the woman did, gluing the furniture onto a piece of construction paper and adding more details with markers.

Say: One of the people that Elisha helped did something special for Elisha. (*Read 2 Kings 4.*) **A woman created a room just for Elisha in her house that he could stay at whenever he wanted. Let's design a room like the woman did. Just like this woman helped Elisha, we can help others too.**

And Now, the News!

Say: There were some pretty amazing things that happened in Elisha's life. Let's read about some of them and create a news broadcast together!

Directions: Check out the Scriptures below and create a newscast video with the kids. Kids pretend to be townspeople getting interviewed or people from the passage itself.

- 2 Kings 2:9–14
- 2 Kings 2:23–25
- 2 Kings 4

Wash and Be Clean

Say: Let's wash like Naaman did in our Bible story. Remember, because of the young servant, Naaman was able to get help. In the same way, **we can help others** too by telling them about God's power.

Directions: Using washable markers, kids carefully draw dots on each other's hands and wrists to represent leprosy. Using a basin of soapy water, kids wash to be clean like Naaman.

Chapter 22: Jonah

BIBLE STORY REFERENCE: Jonah 1:1–17, 2:10, 3:3

MEMORY VERSE: *In my distress I called to the Lord, and he answered me. Jonah 2:2*

**Big Idea
God Loves to Forgive**

Overview

Say: Jonah was a prophet like Elijah and Elisha. He gave messages to people from God. One day, God told Jonah to go to a land called Nineveh. Jonah had heard about these people and he did not like what he heard! These people were terrible. He did not want to go to Nineveh. So he bought a boat ticket to Tarshish instead. But God knows all things and he knew what Jonah was up to. He put a stop to Jonah's escape plan in a very unusual way. (*Open with prayer requests, praises, and a time of prayer.*)

Bible Story

 Say: Have your parents ever told you to do something and you did the exact opposite?

In our Bible story today, Jonah did not obey God. God wanted him to go to Nineveh, but Jonah bought a ticket for a totally different place! How was he going to give God's message to the people if he was headed in the wrong direction? God was not pleased with Jonah's actions. Let's read what happened in Jonah 1:1–17. (*Read Scripture aloud.*) Inside the fish, Jonah thought about what he had done. He told God that he was sorry and he promised to go to Nineveh. **God loves to forgive** and he forgave Jonah for his disobedience. God made the fish spit Jonah out onto dry land (Jonah 2:10). This time, Jonah obeyed God and gave a message to the people of Nineveh. (*Read Jonah 3:3.*)

Outline
Overview
Bible Story
Opening Game
Object Lesson
Additional Optional Activities

Materials
- Bibles
- Reproducible page 228
- 4 sheets of large paper
- Marker
- Red cellophane
- White paper plate
- Pink, yellow, red markers
- Large sheet of poster board
- Large marker
- Masking tape
- Markers or crayons
- Scissors
- Blindfold
- Jonah figure
- Paper
- Fish stickers
- Swedish fish or goldfish crackers

Opening Game: Where Is Nineveh?

Materials
- 4 sheets of large paper

Tip: If the game is too easy for the kids, start by calling out one city and then change it as the kids are running.

Preparation: Label the four walls of the room with these signs: Nineveh, Tarshish, Joppa, and Egypt. Post one sign on each wall of your room.

Say: In today's Bible story, Jonah headed in the wrong direction. He wasn't confused, but in this game—you might end up that way!

Directions: Call out a city. Children run towards the named wall. The last child to touch the "city wall" is out for the round. Keep playing until there are one or two players remaining.

LEARNING TIDBITS
Visual Learners

- Use expressive facial and body movements.
- Use visuals aids. Wall displays, posters, projected images (PowerPoint), flash cards, graphic organizers, models, pictures, physical examples, costumes, etc.
- These learners recognize words by sight and shape.
- They prefer lists and boxes or tables to organize thoughts.
- They recall information by remembering how it looked on a page.

Turn to page 91 for more Learning Tidbits.

Object Lesson: God Forgives Our Sin

Materials

- Red cellophane
- White paper plate
- Pink, yellow, red markers

Optional

- Tape

Say: In our Bible story, Jonah had a job to do. God told him to go to Ninevah. But Jonah did not obey. When we disobey God, what is that called? (*Children respond.*) **That's right, disobeying God is called sin.** (*Write "sin" on the white paper plate with the red marker.*)

In our Bible story, Jonah sinned against God. But he was not the only one who was sinning against God. The people in Nineveh were very wicked as well. They were doing things that were not pleasing to God. God was going to punish them because of their sins, but something interesting happened when Jonah gave the people of Nineveh God's message. (*Read Jonah 3:3–10.*)

The people of Nineveh repented and turned from their evil ways. They told God they were sorry. What kind of sinful things do you think the Ninevites were doing? (*Children respond. With markers write responses on the paper plate.*)

You might be right. But just like Jonah said he was sorry, the people of Nineveh said they were sorry, too. God loves to forgive sins and he forgave the people of Nineveh. (*Cover the paper plate with the red cellophane, taping it to the back to keep it tight if needed.*) **When God forgives our sins, they disappear—** just like the sins on this plate are now gone. I'm so glad that **God loves to forgive** sins. He forgave Jonah, he forgave the people of Nineveh, and he loves to forgive our sins, too.

Lead the kids in silent prayer, confessing any sins silently to God and asking for his forgiveness.

Additional Optional Activities

Reverse Hide and Seek

Directions: This game works best if you can play through several rooms. One person will pretend to be Jonah and hide from the group. The rest of the kids go in search of "Jonah." When a child finds "Jonah," they hide with him. The game continues until everyone has found Jonah.

Say: Jonah tried to hide from God, but that is not possible. God knows all things and sees all things. He knew what Jonah was up to! In this game though, we can hide from each other.

Materials

- Reproducible page 228
- Large sheet of poster board
- Large marker
- Masking tape
- Markers or crayons
- Scissors
- Blindfold

Pin Jonah in the Fish

Preparation: Draw a large fish on sheet of poster board, drawing an X in the middle of the belly. Make copies page 228, one for each child. Make a loop of masking tape for each child.

Say: God put Jonah right where he wanted him— inside a great fish. Let's see if we can do the same!

Directions: Give each child a copy of page 228. Children use markers or crayons to color their "Jonah," cut the figure out, write their name on the back, and place a masking-tape loop on the back. Kids take turns getting blindfolded and trying to get their Jonah on the X inside the big fish. The closest "Jonah" chooses a volunteer to tell a sentence about the Bible story or repeat the Bible verse.

Materials

- Jonah figure from previous activity
- Paper
- Markers or crayons
- Fish stickers
- Swedish fish or goldfish crackers

Fish Stickers and Snack

Say: Let's make a picture based on the Bible story!

Directions: Using the Jonah figure from the previous activity, have kids create an illustration for the story. Kids stick Jonah on paper and draw a big fish and the ocean around him. Place fish stickers on drawing. Kids eat Swedish fish or goldfish crackers while they work.

Chapter 23: Shadrach, Meshach, Abednego

**Big Idea
Friends Help
Make Us
Strong**

BIBLE STORY REFERENCE: Daniel 3:8–29

MEMORY VERSE: *Praise be to the God of Shadrach, Meshach and Abednego, who has sent his angel and rescued his servants! Daniel 3:28*

Overview

Say: Shadrach, Meshach, and Abednego were part of God's special people, but they were no longer living in the land of Israel. They had been taken away to a land called Babylon. In Babylon, the King (named Nebuchadnezzar) did not worship the one true God. He made a rule that all the people in his land had to bow down to a giant golden statue. Shadrach, Meshach, and Abednego were faced with a tough choice, but they stood strong together. (*Open with prayer requests, praises, and a time of prayer.*)

Bible Story

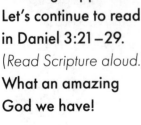

Say: In our Bible story today, three friends were faced with a tough choice. They could bow down to a fake god or they could worship the one true God. They all stood together and did the right thing. Let's read about it in Daniel 3:8–18. (*Read Scripture aloud.*) **Friends help make us strong** and these three friends encouraged each other to do the right thing, even

when it was a scary situation. They were indeed thrown into the furnace, but something amazing happened. Let's continue to read in Daniel 3:21–29. (*Read Scripture aloud.*) What an amazing God we have!

Outline
Overview
Bible Story
Opening Game
Object Lesson
Additional Optional Activities

Materials
- Bibles
- 4 toy people
- 4 cups
- Something heavy
- Camera
- Printer
- Masking tape
- 6 cardboard squares
- Name tags

Opening Game: Mystery Man

Materials

- 4 toy people
- 4 cups

Say: In today's Bible story, Shadrach, Meshach and Abednego were thrown into a blazing fire furnace because they refused to worship a fake god. The king threw three men into the furnace, but when he looked, there was a fourth mystery man in the furnace with the three friends. In this game, you are going to try to find the mystery man.

Directions: Put each toy person under a cup, making it clear to the kids which one will serve as the "Mystery Man." Tell them to try and keep track of the mystery man as you mix up the cups. Swirl around the cups. A volunteer lifts up a cup to find the "mystery man." Give each child three tries. If a child finds the mystery man, they choose a volunteer to tell a sentence about the story. Play again as time permits.

LEARNING TIDBITS
Auditory Learners

- Learn by not only hearing but repeating
- Benefit from reteaching the lesson to someone else
- Are distracted by background noise
- Have difficulty following written directions
- Memorize by repeating out loud
- Song and rhyming help them learn
- Video or audio methods of reinforcement work well
- Learn well by participating in small groups

Turn to page 95 for more Learning Tidbits.

Object Lesson: Let's Lift It Together

Materials

- Something heavy (a stack of books, brick, log, etc.)

Say: In today's Bible story, Shadrach, Meshach, and Abednego stuck together and did the right thing. It must have been hard for them to stand up to the king. (*Read Daniel 3:16–18.*)

What do you think would have happened if one of the friends decided to bow to the statue? (*Children respond.*)

You might be right. It's often harder to do the right thing if the people around us are doing the wrong thing. That's why it's so important to choose friends that will choose to do the right thing along with us. **Friends help make us strong.** Today, we're going to do a little experiment. I need a volunteer.

Directions: Pick one child to come up front and hand them a heavy thing to hold. If possible, have them hold it over their head.

Say: How does it feel to hold this? (*Volunteer responds.*) Is it getting harder to hold? (*Volunteer responds.*) **We can certainly do the right thing on our own. God will help us do that.** But after a little while, sometimes it gets hard, and we need some encouragement and help. That's where our friends come in. I need another volunteer to come help.

Directions: Pick another volunteer. Children hold the heavy object between them at chest level.

Say: How does it feel to hold the heavy thing now? (*Volunteer responds.*) **Friends help make us strong** and can encourage us to do the right thing. Just like the three friends in the Bible helped each other do the right thing, we can encourage each other to stand strong as well.

Additional Optional Activities

Materials
- Camera
- Printer

Tip: Inexpensive black and white posters can be made at office-supply stores.

Bonus Idea: Search online for "ice breaker games for kids" if you need ideas.

Materials
- Masking tape
- 6 cardboard squares

Tip: Time the kids to see how fast they can make it across the "river."

Materials
- Name tags

Group Picture

Say: Just like Shadrach, Meshach, and Abednego helped make each other strong, we can encourage each other to do good things, too. Let's take a picture together to remind ourselves that friends make each other strong.

Directions: Gather kids together and take a group picture. Print the picture. Use the pictures to decorate the room. After the group picture, play some icebreaker games to help kids get to know each other and grow their friendships.

Crossing the River

Preparation: Create a river by making two parallel lines on the ground with masking tape or yarn.

Say: In this game, you must work together in order to cross a "river." Let's help each other and to be an encouragement.

Directions: Give kids six square cardboard "rafts" to use in crossing the river. Kids place a cardboard square down to help each other cross the river. If a raft is left unattended, it will "float away" (An adult will remove.).

A Skit in Babylon

Say: Wasn't that an amazing Bible story? Let's reenact today's Bible story.

Directions: Assign each child a specific character in the story (using name tags helps the kids keep track of their roles). Set up the room with props such as the giant statue and a place for the fiery furnace. Read Daniel 3, encouraging kids to act along as you read. Record the skit with a video camera or phone.

Chapter 24: Daniel

BIBLE STORY REFERENCE: Daniel 6:1–23

MEMORY VERSE: *My God sent his angel, and he shut the mouths of the lions. Daniel 6:22*

Big Idea
God Can Make Me Brave

Overview

Say: Like Shadrach, Meshach, and Abednego, Daniel was a part of God's special people, but he was no longer living in the land of Israel. He was now living in the kingdom of the Medes and Persians. Daniel was one of the king's officials. Like Joseph in Genesis, Daniel could interpret dreams (Daniel 4). He was able to tell the foreign kings about the one true God. In today's Bible story, the king was Darius. King Darius had many officials, but Daniel was his best and his favorite. This made the other officials angry. (*Read Daniel 6:1–5.*) They made a plan to get Daniel in trouble for obeying the one true God. (*Open with prayer requests, praises, and a time of prayer.*)

Bible Story

Say: In our Bible story today, Daniel had a hard choice. King Darius had made a law that stated no one could pray to anyone but the king for 30 days. Daniel knew this was not right. He continued to pray to the one true God. Let's read about it in Daniel 6:10–13. (*Read Scripture aloud.*) When the king's officials told him Daniel had disobeyed the law, the king had no choice but to punish Daniel. Let's keep reading in Daniel 6:14–18. (*Read Scripture aloud.*) Daniel knew he would be thrown into a den of lions, but he did the right thing anyway. Let's read what happened in Daniel 6:19–23. (*Read Scripture aloud.*) **Wow!** God made Daniel brave and **God can make me brave**, too.

Outline
Overview
Bible Story
Opening Game
Object Lesson
Additional Optional Activities

Materials
• Bibles
• Reproducible page 229
• Picture or video of hot air balloons
• 12-inch fleece circles
• Fiberfill
• Permanent marker
• Fine-tipped markers or colored pencils
• Cardstock in various colors
• Markers or crayons

Opening Game: Lions and Daniels

Say: God shut the lions' mouth to protect Daniel. I bet the other officials were even angrier after they found out their plan did not work! In this game, we're going to review the key players by playing a game similar to rock, paper, scissors. Here are the motions:

- **Other officials**: Angry Fists
- **Daniel:** Praying Hands
- **Lions:** Claws and Teeth

Directions: Kids will stand back to back and on the count of three, they will spin around to reveal one of the hand motions. The officials beat Daniel (or so they think!) because they were able to get Daniel thrown in the lion's den. The lion beats the officials (because they ended up with the lions in the end) and Daniel beats the lions (because God rescued Daniel).

LEARNING TIDBITS
Tactile Learners

- Writing or note-taking, and drawing are key elements in processing and remembering
- Hands-on activities like projects and demonstrations are preferred. For younger ones allow them to experience textures and sensory experiences like things that gush between their fingers, water, etc.
- Use board and card games, demonstrations, projects, role plays, etc.
- For older kids, use "while listening and reading" activities. For example, ask students to fill in a table while listening to a talk, or to label a diagram while reading (often referred to as "guided notes").

Turn to page 99 for more Learning Tidbits.

Object Lesson: Power to Rise

Materials

• Picture or video of hot air balloon

Optional: Instead of a picture or video of hot air balloon, bring in an actual floating lantern (available at discount stores, outdoor-living stores, or online)

Say: Has anyone ever seen a hot air balloon (or floating lantern) in real life? What makes it float up in the air?

That's right! The balloon (or lantern) **would just be a floppy mess if it were not for the fire inside of it. The fire heats the air inside the balloon** (or lantern) **and causes it to go up, up, up!**

Directions: Play video of hot air balloon or light lantern and watch it float up.

Say: It's pretty amazing, isn't it? The fire makes the balloon (or lantern) **do incredible things!** In today's Bible story, Daniel was in a scary situation. He knew that if he prayed to the one true God, he would be thrown in a den with lions. Daniel could've crumpled up emotionally and just stopped praying. He could have hidden and not let anyone know that he was praying. But Daniel didn't do either of those things. (*Read Daniel 6:10.*)

Just like this balloon (or lantern), **Daniel had something inside of him that helped him do amazing things. It was God. Just like the fire inside the balloon helps it to do amazing things, God helped Daniel do something amazing. God made Daniel brave and God can make me brave, too. **God can make you brave**. God lifts us up to do things we never thought we could do. He is like the fire inside this balloon.

I'm so glad that **God can make me brave.**

Directions: End with prayer, asking God to make us brave in situations where needed this week.

Materials

- 12-inch fleece circles, one brown and one yellow for each child
- Fiberfill
- Permanent marker

Optional

- Adhesive-backed wiggle eyes

Alternate Idea: Use hot glue gun to attach the eyes.

Materials

- Reproducible page 229
- Fine-tipped markers or colored pencils

Materials

- Cardstock in various colors
- Markers or crayons

Bonus Idea: Hole punch the notecards and put them on a small metal ring or tuck them inside a small cardboard box (available at discount stores).

Lion Pillow

Directions: Use two pieces of fleece to create a lion pillow. Start by cutting two 12-inch circles, one from brown fleece and one from yellow. Cut slits in each circle, starting on the outside and going about 4 inches in towards the center. The slits should be about 2 inches apart. Place the circles on top of each other and tie the slits together (one of each color for each knot). Leave four fringe pieces untied to allow for stuffing. Stuff lion with fiberfill. Finish tying the fringe. Add eyes, mouth, and whiskers with a permanent marker. Optional: With adult help, use hot glue gun to glue on wiggle eyes.

Say: Daniel faced a den of lions, but just like these crafts, the lions ended up being harmless (by God's power!).

Coloring Page

Preparation: Copy the page 229, making one for each child.

Say: As we color, let's talk about ways we might need God to help them to be brave this upcoming week.

Directions: Children use fine-tipped markers or colored pencils to color the lion on the reproducible page.

Prayer Cards

Say: Prayer was important to Daniel. Prayer is an amazing thing! Let's make a project that will help us to pray throughout the week.

Directions: Kids write prayers on notecards so they can practice prayer throughout the week. Brainstorm some prayers to write down (pre-writers can draw pictures). Remember to include leaders, those who are sick, friends, and family members. Add some praises as well.

Chapter 25: Esther

BIBLE STORY REFERENCE: Esther 2:15–18, 3:6–16

MEMORY VERSE: *Who knows but that you have come to your royal position for such a time as this? Esther 4:14*

Big Idea
God Has a Plan

Overview

Say: Esther was a Jewish girl. She was part of God's special people. Like many of the Israelite people though, she was no longer living in God's special land. Esther was living in Persia. In the book of Esther, there are many surprising twists and turns. We see clearly that God has a plan by making Esther the queen. Because of her royal position, she is able to influence the king and save her people from destruction. Sometimes, in our own lives, it is hard to make sense of things, but we can rest in knowing that **God has a plan—** always! *(Open with prayer requests, praises, and a time of prayer.)*

Bible Story

Say: The king of Persia was in need of a new queen. He had ladies from all over the land come to the palace so he could choose a new queen. It would be unusual for the king to choose a Jewish girl, but that's just what he did. Let's read about it in Esther 2:15–18. *(Read Scripture aloud.)* While she was queen, she had an amazing opportunity to save her people from an evil man named Haman. Even though it was forbidden to go to the king uninvited, that's just what Esther had to do. Let's keep reading in Esther 3:6–16. *(Read Scripture aloud.)* **God has a plan** and the Jewish people were saved by Esther's brave actions.

Outline
Overview
Bible Story
Opening Game
Object Lesson
Additional Optional Activities

Materials
- Bibles
- Reproducible page 230
- Reproducible page 231
- Noise makers or musical instruments
- Drinking straws
- Marbles
- Glue
- Hamantaschen
- Plastic masks
- Craft supplies
- Camera or cell phone
- Printer

Opening Game: Let's Make Some Noise!

Materials

- Reproducible page 230
- Noise makers or rhythm instruments

Say: The story of Esther is very important to the Jewish people. There is a special celebration each year called *Purim* to remember Esther and what she did for her people. During this celebration, kids dress up in masks and play games.

One favorite part of this tradition is reading aloud the Bible story of Esther. In this story, Haman is the bad guy. Any time the name *Haman* is mention, kids make noise with noisemakers, instruments, clapping, stomping their feet, or by shouting.

Are you ready to make some noise? In the Bible story of Esther, Haman is the bad guy. I'm going to read the story of Esther to you and every time you hear the bad guy's name, I want you to make some noise! Use these noisemakers, instruments, clap, stomp your feet, or even shout!

Directions: Read story from page 230, encouraging children to make noise whenever you read the name *Haman.*

LEARNING TIDBITS
Kinesthetic Learners

- Action is important
- Need to "do something" as a key part of instruction or learning
- Sitting still for long periods is hard
- Use movement as a memory aid—hand signs to memory verse
- Use physical activities, competitions, board games, role plays, etc.
- Skits or acting out the story.
- Intersperse activities which requires students to sit quietly with activities that allow them to move around and be active

These are also the children that respond well to participating in community service. Statistics show that once a child physically participates in something they are more committed to it.

Turn to page 103 for more Learning Tidbits.

Object Lesson: Through the Maze

Materials
• Reproducible page 231

Bonus Idea: Children divide into pairs. Blindfold one child in each pair and have the other child instruct them around the room without them hitting anything or touching them.

Say: God guides us when we don't know what will happen next.

Preparation: Copy page 231, making one for each child.

Directions: Children use pencils to help Esther find her way through the maze.

Say: Often when we do a maze, we take a few wrong turns along the way. One way might seem right, but it ends up at a dead end! There is a path from the beginning of the maze to the end of the maze, but it's not always easy to figure out right away.

That's how life is, too. **God has a plan** for each of our lives. He has a path from the beginning of our lives to the end of our lives, but things sometimes look like a maze for a while.

Esther must have wondered what God's plan was when she became queen. God allowed Esther to be queen so that she could save her people. There may have been some strange twists and turns in the story of Esther, but it was clear that God had a plan all along. (*Read Esther 4:9–14.*)

God's plan didn't make sense to Esther. No one was supposed to go to the king uninvited! It seemed like a wrong turn in a maze, but it was what God wanted her to do.

Esther prayed about her decision and then approached the king. God rewarded Esther's courage and saved the Jewish people from destruction.

I am so glad that God has a plan for each and every one of us. Even when life seems like a twisty maze, I know that God is in control and that God has a plan.

Additional Optional Activities

Materials

- Drinking straws
- Marbles
- Glue

Bonus Idea: to build a 3-D maze that the kids can walk through, use pool noodles on the ground.

Materials

- Hamantaschen (available at bakeries)

Alternate idea: Look online for a recipe or tutorial on how to make these traditional cookies.

Materials

- Plastic masks, available at party-supply stores
- Craft supplies (glue, tape, paint pens, crayons, markers, ribbons, sequins, stickers, feathers, faux jewels, etc.)
- Camera or cell phone
- Printer

Make a Maze

Say: Even though a maze looks like a jumble of lines, there is always a way through. This reminds us that even though things sometimes look confusing, **God has a plan.** Let's try to build our own maze.

Directions: Children build mazes. A marble maze can be built by gluing drinking straws onto the lid of a shoe box. Who can build the most complicated maze? Give the kids some space to work and encourage some creative thinking!

Bake Some Cookies

Say: In the celebration of Esther, it is a tradition to make Hamantaschen. Let's eat some together.

Directions: In the Jewish celebration of Purim, cookies are made in the shape of a triangle to represent Haman's hat. The cookies are called Hamantaschen.

Masquerade

Say: Another tradition in the Purim celebration is making masks. Let's make some together.

Directions: Provide simple plastic masks for the kids to embellish. Paper plates, cut in half, can also be used (hole punch the sides and use elastic to hold on the masks). Be sure to provide plenty of craft supplies for children to use in decorating their masks. Take pictures of kids in their masks. Print and display photos for all to see.

Chapter 26: The Prophets

BIBLE STORY REFERENCE: Isaiah 53:4–6, 2 Timothy 3:16

MEMORY VERSE: *Call to me and I will answer you and tell you great and unsearchable things you do not know. Jeremiah 33:3*

Big Idea
God Speaks to His People

Overview

Say: God sent many messages to his people, the Israelites, over the years. He sent messages to them when they were living in Israel and Judah. He sent messages when they were living in Babylon. And he sent messages to them when they were living in Persia. Usually, God sent messages through his prophets. A prophet is a special messenger from God. Many of the prophets told the people to turn from their wicked ways and worship the one true God again (Jeremiah 35:15). Other prophets told about the coming Savior, God's son, who would save the people from their sins (Isaiah 53:4–6). God continues to speak to his people today, but in different ways. God most often speaks through the Bible, his written Word. (*Open with prayer requests, praises, and a time of prayer.*)

Outline
Overview
Bible Story
Opening Game
Object Lesson
Additional Optional Activities

Materials
- **Bibles**
- **Paper**
- **Children's worship music and player**
- **Notebooks**
- **Pen or markers**
- **Poster board sheets**
- **Markers, crayons, or colored pencils**
- **Stickers**

Bible Story

Say: Have you ever received a letter or a card in the mail? (*Children respond.*)

It's exciting to get a message from a friend or family member. Sometimes the note will tell us that a person is thinking about us. Sometimes the message is about some recent news or an event coming up. The Bible is like a note from God to us. Let's read 2 Timothy 3:16. (*Read Scripture aloud.*) **God speaks to his people** through the Bible. Certain verses remind us that God loves us and has a plan for our lives. Certain verses tell us how to live and how to make God happy. I'm glad that we can hear from God anytime we read the Bible.

Opening Game: Pass the Note

Materials

- Paper
- Children's worship music and player

Preparation: Print the words of the verse, Jeremiah 33:3, on a piece of paper. Fold paper in half. Fold three or four other papers in half.

Directions: Kids sit in a circle. Hand each of the folded papers to a child. Play music as kids pass the pieces of paper to the child on their right. After a few moments, stop the music and choose a volunteer to guess who has "the message from God." Named child opens paper to see if it is the paper with the verse. If it is, child reads, or chooses a volunteer, to read the message. If the named child has a blank paper, choose another volunteer to guess. Play again as time permits.

Say: Every verse in the Bible is a message from God. God loves it when we read his words to us. **God speaks to his people** and the Bible is full of his messages to us.

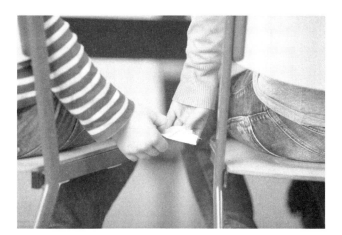

LEARNING TIDBITS
The Five Senses—Taste

- Give the children an opportunity to experience a flavor that may appear in a story. (Unleavened bread, dates, nuts, fish, salt, regional or cultural foods, etc.) Check the Bible story for ideas.
- Be sure to let parents know if you will offer something so they can let you know about allergies.

Turn to page 107 for more about The Five Senses.

Object Lesson: God Speaks

Materials

- Bible

Say: Who has a Bible of their very own? Where did you get the Bible? (*Children respond.*)

A Bible is the most important book ever because it contains the very words of God. God told men what to write in the Bible and they obeyed God. Now we have a whole book full of messages from God about the things he has done and the way that he wants us to live.

God has spoken to his people throughout time.

- God spoke to Abraham when he gave him the promise about a special child.

- God spoke to Joseph through a dream about the sun, moon, and stars.

- God spoke to Moses through a burning bush.

- God spoke to Jonah and told him to go to Nineveh.

God spoke to his people through the prophets for many years. Some of the prophets were named Joel, Amos, Hosea, Jeremiah, Isaiah, Micah, and Malachi. The messages that God gave these prophets are written down in the Bible.

Does anyone have a special Bible they would like to share with the class? (*Kids show others their Bibles. If you have access to specialty or unique Bibles, bring one or more to show the kids.*)

There are lots of different types of Bibles—different colors, different pictures, or different designs on the cover. Some Bibles have study tips or devotionals inside of them. But the most important part of any Bible is God's words.

Additional Optional Activities

Materials

- Notebooks
- Pen or markers

Journaling to God

Say: God speaks to his people through the Bible, but we can write to God as well. Journaling often helps us focus our thoughts and it gives us a great way to remember our developing relationship with God.

Directions: Provide kids with notebooks and some fun writing utensils and encourage them to write a letter to God. It could be about something they are worried about, something they are happy about, or something they want to tell God about. If kids seem to enjoy this practice, try to include a time of journaling to God each week.

Prayer Time

Say: God speaks to his people, both through Scripture and through prayer. Let's spend a few quiet minutes talking with God.

Directions: Encourage kids to spend some quiet time in prayer. Have kids spread out throughout the room. Children spend four or five minutes in silence as they seek to spend time with God. After, volunteers share about their experience.

My Favorite Verse

Preparation: Cut poster board in half, making one half-sheet for each child.

Say: God often uses Bible verses that we have memorized to speak to our hearts. Let's make a poster to help us memorize a favorite verse.

Directions: Kids create a decorative poster of a favorite memory verse. If they are having trouble thinking of a verse, mark some verses in Bibles to get them started. Children use markers, crayons, colory pencils and stickers to decorate their posters. Encourage children to place their poster in their room to remember the verse.

Materials

- Poster board sheet, one for every two children
- Markers, crayons, or colored pencils
- Stickers

Chapter 27: Time of Waiting

BIBLE STORY REFERENCE: Galatians 4:4–5

MEMORY VERSE: *You see, at just the right time, when we were still powerless, Christ died for the ungodly. Romans 5:6*

Big Idea
God Sometimes Makes Us Wait

Overview

Say: From the beginning of time, God had a plan in place to rescue people from their sins, but it took a long time for that plan to come to pass. God knows all things. He knows what is best for us, and **God sometimes makes us wait.** God made his special people wait a very long time for the Savior to come. In fact, not only did they have to wait, but they did not get any messages from God for over 400 years. They must have felt like giving up! Would the promised Savior ever come? (*Open with prayer requests, praises, and a time of prayer.*)

Bible Story

Say: Have you ever had to wait for something exciting to happen? (*Children respond.*)

That's how things were for the Israelites. They knew that God was going to send a Savior to rescue them from their sins, but they weren't sure when it was going to happen. They had to wait a long time, without any messages from God. God was waiting for the perfect time. Let's read Galatians 4:4–5 and Romans 5:6. (*Read Scriptures aloud.*) It's hard for us to understand God's timing (Ecclesiastes 3:1), but we can rest assured that even when **God sometimes makes us wait,** his timing is always best.

Outline
Overview
Bible Story
Opening Game
Object Lesson
Additional Optional Activities

Materials
- **Bibles**
- **Reproducible page 232**
- **Kitchen timer**
- **Hourglass**
- **Scissors**
- **Paper plates**
- **Brads**
- **Markers or crayons**
- **Colored sand**
- **Funnels**
- **Spoons**
- **Small plastic bottles**

Opening Game: Time's Up!

Materials

- Kitchen timer

Tip: If the game seems too easy for the kids, hide two or three timers at once to increase the challenge.

Say: The Israelites didn't have a timer for when Jesus would come to Earth. They had no idea when he would arrive. In this game though, you do have a timer and it's about to go off! Your job is to find the timer before it beeps.

Directions: Set a kitchen timer for three or four minutes and hide it somewhere in the room. Kids will listen for the ticking noise and try to find the timer before it dings.

LEARNING TIDBITS
The Five Senses—Smell

- Try to find a way to incorporate smells into your lesson or the environment.
- Think about how the smell of sunscreen can make you think of days of enjoyment on the beach, or the smell of baked goods taking you back to memories of home.
- Smell is a powerful tool to help children recall an event or a story.
- You can use scents, essential oils, scratch and sniff stickers, scented play dough, or bring in an object that has a smell. A can of tuna or stinky shells from the ocean when talking about fishing or fishermen stories, Jonah, etc.

Turn to page 111 for Bible Tidbits.

Object Lesson: Waiting

Materials

- Hourglass (the bigger the better)

Say: Have you ever used an hourglass? (*Children respond.*) Depending on how much sand is in the hourglass, it can seem like a really long time before it gets from one end to the other. All the sand has to go through this little tiny hole. Sometimes we can make it a little faster by shaking it, but the sand still has to go through the hole, so there's still a lot of waiting!

It was sort of that way for Jesus' arrival, too. Everything had to be in place before Jesus' arrived.

God wanted the whole world to hear about the good news of salvation, so he was waiting for just the right time to send Jesus. We call this the fullness of time. By the time Jesus arrived on Earth, there was a reliable road system (thanks to Rome) and a common language (thanks to the Greeks).

This allowed people to tell each other about the good news of Jesus quickly. It must have been hard for God's people to wait all that time for Jesus' to arrive. **God sometimes makes us wait,** too. Sometimes we ask God to heal someone we love, but he doesn't do it right away. Sometimes we ask God for a new toy or new clothes. Sometimes God says yes. Sometimes God says no. And sometimes God makes us wait. We can trust God to do what is best for our lives, even if it means waiting.

Additional Optional Activities

Materials

- Reproducible page 232
- Scissors
- Paper plates, one for each child
- Brads, one for each child
- Markers or crayons

Optional

- Number stickers (1 – 12), one set for each child

Alternate Idea: Give each child an embroidery hoop with burlap inside. Using large plastic needles, have the kids stitch on buttons for the numbers around the clock.

Materials

- None

Materials

- Colored sand
- Funnels
- Spoons
- Small plastic bottles

Clock Craft

Preparation: For each child, make a copy of page 232.

Say: God sometimes makes us wait. Let's make a craft that reminds us that even though God sometimes makes us wait, his timing is always best.

Directions: Give each child a copy of page 232. Children cut out circle, arrows, and Big Idea. Children then glue circle to plate and Big Idea onto clock circle. Children push brads through the ends of the arrows and into the center of the circle on the plate, bend back the brads to lock arrows in place but keep brad loose enough for arrows to rotate. Children write numbers around the circle like a clock. If you have number stickers, children place them on the circle in the correct order.

How Long Can You Wait?

Say: The Israelites had to wait a long time before they heard anything from God. In this game, let's see how long you can wait without laughing or talking.

Directions: Kids pair up and stare each other in the eyes (blinking is allowed). How long can they wait without looking away? How long can they wait without laughing or talking? The child who holds out longest tells, or chooses a volunteer to tell a sentence about the Bible story.

Sand Art

Say: Just like we learned about with the sand timer, **God sometimes makes us wait.** Let's make an art project with sand to remind us of the lesson today.

Directions: Place a funnel in the plastic bottle. Have children scoop sand and pour into the funnel. Encourage kids to make sand art, layering different colors of sand in their bottles.

Chapter 28: Jesus Is Born

BIBLE STORY REFERENCE: Luke 2:4–15

MEMORY VERSE: *Today in the town of David a Savior has been born to you; he is the Messiah, the Lord. Luke 2:11*

Overview

Say: From the beginning of time, God had a plan in place to rescue people from their sins, but the plan wasn't always clear to God's people. God was sending his Son, Jesus to pay the price for all the sin of the world. **Jesus' birth was the big event**. All the things God did in the Old Testament were getting ready for Jesus' arrival. That's a pretty big deal. I'm so glad God had a plan, and that he is powerful enough to make it happen. (*Open with prayer requests, praises, and a time of prayer.*)

Bible Story

Say: Usually, a big event takes a lot of planning and work to get everything ready. A country spends years getting ready for the Olympics. Just imagine all the things God had to put in place for the really big event: Jesus' birth! Long before Jesus came, God told the world what was going to

happen. Let's read about it in Isaiah 9:6. (*Read Scripture aloud.*) Finally, at just the right time, Jesus was born. Let's turn in the Bible now to Luke 2:4–7. (*Read Scripture aloud.*) God celebrated the big event with a concert of angels! Let's read Luke 2:13. (*Read Scripture aloud.*) What an amazing sight! **Jesus' birth was the big event** because it was the fulfillment of God's rescue plan. Jesus came to save us from our sins. What good news!

Outline
Overview
Bible Story
Opening Game
Object Lesson
Additional Optional Activities

Materials
- Bibles
- Reproducible page 233
- Index cards
- Tickets to a special event
- Scissors
- Resealable plastic bags
- Name tags
- Measuring cups
- Flour
- Salt
- Water
- Bowl
- Spoon
- Rolling pin
- Star cookie cutters
- Drinking straw or chopstick

Opening Game: Go Tell the News!

Materials

- Bible
- Index cards

Say: As soon as the shepherds heard the good news about Jesus, they visited the newborn Savior. Then, they told everyone they saw about the good news. (*Read Luke 2:17–18.*) **In this game, we're going to see how fast we can spread the good news, too!**

Directions: Writing each child's name on an index card. Scramble the cards and pass them out to the kids, making sure no one gets their own name. Spread the kids out in a large room or outside. Tell one child some "good news" (for example, Jesus is born!). As soon as they

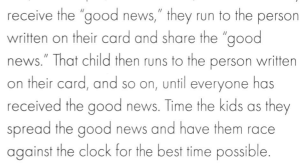

receive the "good news," they run to the person written on their card and share the "good news." That child then runs to the person written on their card, and so on, until everyone has received the good news. Time the kids as they spread the good news and have them race against the clock for the best time possible.

LEARNING TIDBITS

- The Bible was written over 1600 years from 1500 B.C. to 100 A.D.
- There are sixty-six books in the Bible divided into chapters and verses (thirty-nine Old Testament books; twenty-seven New Testament Books).
- There are five books not divided by chapters—Obadiah, Philemon, 2 John, 3 John, and Jude.
- The longest chapter in a book of the Bible is in Psalms (176 verses).
- The longest book is Psalms (150 chapters).
- The shortest book is Psalm 117. (This book is also at the physical center of the Bible.)

Turn to page 115 for more Bible Tidbits.

Object Lesson: What a Special Event

Materials

• Tickets to a special event

Tip: You could get tickets to upcoming church events or a flyer.

Say: Who can tell me what these are? (*Children respond.*) Tickets! These are tickets to a special event. (*If this is an event you personally attended, tell the kids a little bit about it—including things the host might have had to do to get ready for the event.*)

Whenever there is a big event in our lives, we usually have to wait a little bit before we can go, right? Sometimes we see signs or billboards advertising the special event or sometimes we hear our friends talking about the event as it is coming up.

It was the same way with God's chosen people. They had to wait for a big event—Jesus' birth! They knew it was coming because God's prophets had told them about it. People probably often wondered when God's promised Savior was coming. Do you think they talked about it a lot as they waited? (*Children respond.*)

Just like a big event, there were a lot of things God had to do to get ready. Jesus' birth was a really big deal! He was going to save all the people of the world—including you and me—from the penalty for their sins (Romans 6:23).

The cool thing is, Jesus' birth was really just the start of the big event for Christians. When we accept Jesus' free gift of salvation, we get to be friends with God forever. We can grow in our relationship with him and get to know him better every single day.

So, **Jesus' birth was the big event**, but the big event doesn't have to end for us! We can keep celebrating Jesus' birth, life, death, and resurrection every single day. Jesus' birth was part of God's plan to save us from the penalty for our sins and to have a relationship with us forever. That's pretty exciting news!

Materials
- Reproducible page 233
- Scissors
- Resealable plastic bags

Alternate Idea: Place magnetic paper on the back of each cut out (available online or at office supply stores) so kids can play with them on the refrigerator at home.

Materials
- Name tags

Optional: Provide robes and props to take the fun over the top!

Materials
- Measuring cups
- Flour
- Salt
- Water
- Bowl
- Spoon
- Rolling pin
- Star cookie cutters
- Drinking straw

Alternate Idea: Use air-dry modeling clay instead of making Salt Dough.

Tip: Make a few extra ornaments to have for new children that may come next week. That way they can paint them with the rest of the class.

Nativity

Preparation: Copy page 233, making one for each child.

Say: Let's recreate the big event with these figures. Then, put the figures in your plastic bag. You can use them to share the good news of Jesus with others!

Directions: Give each child a copy of the reproducible page to cut out. Children recreate the "big event" of Jesus' birth.

Act It Out

Say: Many of you might have heard the Christmas story before. Now is your chance to take part in it! Let's act out the story as I read it out loud.

Directions: The Christmas story is a familiar Bible story for many kids. Assign each child a role in the story (giving name tags with Bible names helps everyone keep track of roles). Reading from Luke 2 (or a children's Bible storybook), encourage kids to act along with the Bible story as you read out loud.

Starry Salt Dough

Say: One way God told the world about the big event of Jesus' birth was with a special star in the sky. Let's make some star ornaments together!

Directions: Kids make stars from salt dough (recipe below) using cookie cutters. Using a drinking straw or chopstick, make a small hole in the top of each star for hanging later.

Say: Next week, after the dough has dried, we will paint the stars to make ornaments!

Salt Dough Ornaments: 1 cup flour, ½ cup salt, and ½ cup water. Mix ingredients together. Roll out onto table with rolling pin. Use cookie cutters to cut out ornaments. Leave overnight to dry or put in oven at 250°F for one hour. Recipe makes about twenty ornaments. Recipe can easily be doubled.

Chapter 29: Wise Men Visit Jesus

BIBLE STORY REFERENCE: Matthew 2:9–11

MEMORY VERSE: *When they saw the star, they were overjoyed. On coming to the house, they saw the child with his mother Mary, and they bowed down and worshiped him. Matthew 2:10–11*

Big Idea
God Told the World about Jesus

Overview

Say: The news about Jesus' birth was so exciting! God wanted to spread the news right away. God had already told the world that Jesus was coming through the prophets in the Old Testament. Now, **God told the world about Jesus** being born through angels and a special star. He told shepherds in a field about the birth of his Son with a crowd of angels, singing and praising God. The wise men, however, saw a star in the sky that had never been there before. *(Open with prayer requests, praises, and a time of prayer.)*

Bible Story

Say: The wise men from the East spent a lot of time studying a lot of things. They were able to tell when a new star appeared and they knew it meant something special. They followed the star until they reached the house where Jesus and his parents lived. Let's turn in the Bible to Matthew 2:9–11. *(Read Scripture aloud.)* **God told the world about Jesus** in many special ways and now we can tell the world about Jesus, too!

Materials
- **Bibles**
- **Bonus Activity: Reproducible page 234**
- **Objects for an obstacle course**
- **Blindfold**
- **Yellow, gold, or silver construction paper**
- **Scissors**
- **Star books**
- **Black construction paper**
- **Star stickers**
- **Dried dough stars**
- **Paint of various colors**
- **Glitter**
- **Yarn**
- **Frankincense**
- **Myrrh**

Opening Game: Directions, Please?

Materials
- Objects for an obstacle course
- Blindfold

Tip: The "Hidden Star" game from Chapter 1: Creation would also work well for this lesson.

Preparation: Set up a small obstacle course for the kids to walk through. Completing the course should take about 30 seconds. Use chairs, cones, stuffed animals, stacks of books, etc.—even small objects can work.

Directions: Blindfold one child and allow another volunteer to "give them directions" through the obstacle course. Time them to see how long it takes to make it through. Continue with pairs of volunteers completing the course as time allows.

Say: On the wise men's journey, they had to travel mostly at night so they could watch the special star in the sky. It's not easy traveling through a desert at night! In this game, we're going to pretend we are wise men and try to get through this obstacle course as quickly as possible, all while being blindfolded.

LEARNING TIDBITS

- The word *testament* means covenant or contract.
- The Holy Bible is the only one which claims to be the actual words of God.
- Secular historians also wrote about events in the Bible—Josephus, Tacitus, plus many, many more.
- 40 different people wrote the Bible. Paul is credited by most to have written thirteen or fourteen books and Moses wrote five.
- The Bible is in over 2000 languages and dialects.

Turn to page 119 for more Bible Tidbits.

Object Lesson: Looking for the Star

Materials

- Yellow, gold, or silver construction paper
- Scissors

Bonus Idea: Plug in a star that lights up, such as a tree-topper.

Preparation: Cut a star from construction paper.

Say: Has anyone ever seen a shooting star or meteor shower? (*Children respond.*) It's pretty amazing to see God's power on display like that.

God told the world about Jesus through a special star. The wise men must have been very excited to see a new star in the sky. We're not sure how they knew it was a star for the king of the Jews, but they did. Perhaps they studied Jewish prophecies. However they discovered this special fact, they were not going to waste an opportunity to meet this special king.

Do you think you would be willing to pack up everything and follow a star, even though you didn't know where you were headed? (*Children respond.*)

How do you think the wise men (or Magi) were feeling about their journey? (*Children respond.*) You might be right. They might have been feeling all of those things.

One thing we do know for sure, they were overjoyed to find Jesus and his family (Matthew 2:9–11). They brought special gifts for Jesus including gold, frankincense, and myrrh.

God told the world about Jesus through angels and a special star when Jesus was born. God continued to tell the world about Jesus throughout the New Testament and **God wants us to tell the world about Jesus, too**. Jesus coming to Earth is super good news!

Additional Optional Activities

Materials

- Star books
- Black construction paper
- Star stickers

Bonus Idea: Use a cell-phone application that shows what stars are above you right now. Type "stars" and "constellations" into the search engine of an app store. They even show satellites.

Materials

- Dried dough stars, from Chapter 28: Jesus Is Born
- Paint of various colors
- Glitter
- Yarn

Optional: Provide smocks or adult shirts for children to wear while they paint.

Materials

- Frankincense (resin or oil)
- Myrrh (resin or oil)

Tip: Instead of buying these, ask anyone into essential oils at your church if they have any. You only need to borrow them for the smell. Then you can give them back.

Constellations

Directions: Explore the constellations with the kids. Get some books from the library or online about constellations. Kids recreate constellations with star stickers and black construction paper.

Say: The wise men must have spent a lot of time studying the stars. Isn't it cool that we can spot these star formations no matter where we are in the world?

Star Salt Dough

Say: God told the world about Jesus with a special star in the sky. Let's finish the ornaments we started last week.

Directions: Kids paint the dough stars, and use glitter to really bring some sparkle into the project. Loop a piece of yarn through the holes in the stars for hanging.

Smell Those Spices

Say: The wise men brought costly gifts to the new king, Jesus. Let's take a closer look at how these gifts might have looked and smelled.

Directions: Most kids are familiar with gold, but they may not have experienced the scents of frankincense and myrrh. You can find these scents in essential oils or incense. Bring in a few samples for the kids to smell.

Turn to page 234 for a bonus activity

Chapter 30: John the Baptist

BIBLE STORY REFERENCE: Matthew 3:1–13

MEMORY VERSE: *In those days John the Baptist came, preaching in the wilderness of Judea and saying, "Repent, for the kingdom of heaven has come near." Matthew 3:1–2*

Overview

Say: Jesus was born! The big event had come! The shepherds had visited Jesus and so had the wise men. Many people had heard about Jesus as he grew. However, Jesus' birth and childhood was just the beginning. **God prepared the way for his Son** to be the Savior of the world since the beginning of time. John the Baptist was part of God's preparations. *(Open with prayer requests, praises, and a time of prayer.)*

Bible Story

Say: God wanted John the Baptist to tell everyone about Jesus. Let's read Matthew 3:1–6, 11. *(Read Scripture aloud.)* God wanted the people to prepare their hearts to meet Jesus. John the Baptist was Jesus' cousin, but he was kind of a strange character. He wore strange clothes and ate strange things. Nonetheless, he was part of God's plan as **God prepared the way for his Son.** One day, when John was telling people about Jesus, Jesus himself came for a visit! Let's read about it in Matthew 3:13–17. *(Read Scripture aloud.)* **Wow!** God wanted the people to know that Jesus was his Son. This was another way that God prepared the way for his Son.

Outline

Overview
Bible Story
Opening Game
Object Lesson
Additional Optional Activities

Materials

- Bibles
- Reproducible page 235
- Reproducible page 236
- Large basket
- Variety of clothes
- Iced cake
- Mixing bowl
- Cake ingredients
- Paper plates
- Plastic forks
- Napkins
- Cake cutter
- Yarn
- Scissors
- Hole puncher
- Markers or crayons
- Burlap scraps
- Glue

Opening Game: Crazy Clothes Relay

Materials

- Large basket
- Variety of clothes (oversized shirts, capes, shoes, long socks, hats, etc)

Say: John the Baptist wore some pretty crazy clothes, and ate some pretty crazy things. In this game, we're going to put on some fun clothes as we race to complete a relay as a team.

Directions: Fill a laundry basket full of funny clothes for each team. At the start of the race, the first team member will run down, put on an article of clothing and race back to tag the next person in line, relay race style. When everyone on a team has successfully put on an article of crazy clothing and returned to their team line, that team repeats the memory verse or tells a sentence about the story.

LEARNING TIDBITS

- In the Old Testament, Job is the oldest book written by an unknown author about 1500 B.C. The youngest book is Malachi written 400 B.C.
- In the New Testament the oldest book is James written in A.D. 45. The youngest book is Revelation written in A.D. 95.
- Languages of the Bible are Hebrew, Aramaic, and Greek.
- Oldest person to live was Methuselah. He lived to be 969 years old.

Turn to page 123 for Volunteer Tidbits.

Object Lesson: Preparing a Cake

Materials

- Iced cake
- Mixing bowl
- Cake ingredients
- Paper plates
- Plastic forks
- Napkins
- Cake cutter

Preparation: Hide iced cake in the classroom.

Say: (*Hold up mixing bowl and box of cake mix.*) Does anyone want to take a guess at what these things could help me make? (*Children respond.*)

The thing that I am making takes some preparation. There are certain ingredients that need to be just right. I need to mix them in a certain order, being careful not to forget anything! Then, I need to bake this thing for a certain amount of time.

If you guessed a cake, you are right! With these ingredients, I'm preparing to make a cake. After this cake is all baked, I'll put something special on the top—icing! This whole process reminds me a lot of our Scripture Bible story today. God prepared the way for his Son for many years, by creating a special family and giving them a special land to live in. He taught the Israelites what it means to be God's special people and he promised them that there would someday be a Savior to take away the sins of the world. This was all how God prepared the way for his Son. It is similar to how we bake a cake!

John the Baptist was kind of like the icing on the cake. The preparations had all been made—Jesus was born! He was here on Earth. Now, John wanted to make sure everyone knew about the coming Savior, so he was spending his time telling people and helping them to get ready for Jesus through baptism—a way of showing that you repent of your sins and want to live a new life.

Of course, Jesus' coming to Earth is a much bigger deal than just baking a cake, but I think a cake is a perfect way to celebrate the fact that **God prepared the way for his Son!**

Directions: Bring out the hidden, iced cake, plates, forks, napkins, and cake cutter. Cut everyone a slice in celebration of Jesus.

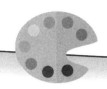

Baptism

Say: John the Baptist wanted the people to repent, or turn away from their sins. Baptism is a way to symbolize a new style of life—following after Christ. Let's talk more about baptism.

Directions: This is a great opportunity to explain the concept of baptism a little more to the kids in your group. Invite an elder or pastor to share with the kids or see if your church has literature on the subject.

Holy Spirit, Like a Dove

Preparation: Copy page 235, making one for each child. Cut yarn into 12-inch lengths, making one length for each child.

Say: After Jesus was baptized, God said from Heaven that he was pleased with his Son. The Bible tells us that something like a dove came from heaven. Let's make a craft that reminds us of this event.

Directions: Give each child a copy of page 235. Children glue the dove to a paper plate, cut out the dove, and then use hole puncher to punch a hole in the middle of the back of the bird. Give them each a piece of yarn to string through the hole and hang the bird at home.

Camel Hair Clothes

Preparation: Copy page 236, making one for each child.

Say: God prepared the way for his Son through the teaching of John the Baptist. Let's dress John in some camel hair clothes.

Directions: Children color picture and glue burlap scraps to John's coat.

Materials
- Reproducible page 235
- Yarn
- Scissors
- Paper plates, one for each child
- Hole puncher

Bonus Idea: For added interest, provide feathers to glue to the dove.

Materials
- Reproducible page 236
- Markers or crayons
- Burlap scraps
- Glue

Bonus Idea: If time permits, draw a scene around John the Baptist, based on the Bible story.

Chapter 31: Jesus Heals the Sick

BIBLE STORY REFERENCE: Mark 2:1–12

MEMORY VERSE: *I tell you, get up, take your mat and go home. Mark 2:11*

Overview

Say: After Jesus was baptized by John the Baptist, he began to tell everyone about the good news of God. Jesus was powerful and he did amazing things called miracles. A miracle is something that cannot be explained by nature or science. It is something only God can do. Jesus did many miracles including changing water into wine (John 2) and healing many people who were sick. In today's Bible story, we will learn about one man who Jesus healed. (*Open with prayer requests, praises, and a time of prayer.*)

Bible Story

Say: Have you ever had a friend who was sick? What kind of things did you do to help that friend feel better? (*Children respond.*)

There are a lot of things we can do to help a sick friend. In today's Bible story, we read about a man who could not walk. People did not have wheelchairs back in the time of Jesus' so this man had to be carried by his friends. Let's read what happened in Mark 2:1–12. These friends knew that **God can heal,** so they decided to do whatever it took to get their friend to Jesus.

Outline
Overview
Bible Story
Opening Game
Object Lesson
Additional Optional Activities

Materials
- **Bibles**
- **2 sturdy blankets**
- **Garden shovel**
- **Cardboard**
- **Craft sticks**
- **Yarn**
- **Poseable toy man**
- **Construction paper**
- **Markers, pens, pencils**
- **Teddy Graham crackers**
- **Frosting**
- **Plastic knives**

Opening Game: Get Him to Jesus!

Materials

- 2 sturdy blankets

Say: In our Bible story, a man needed healing from Jesus. He could not get to Jesus on his own, so four of his friends helped carry him to Jesus. In this game, we're going to work as teams to "race to Jesus."

Directions: Divide the group of kids up into two teams. Give each team a sturdy blanket. Spread the blanket out and have one child lie down on the blanket. The rest of the team should grab the edges of the blanket and prepare to "carry the paralyzed friend." On your signal, teams will pick up the corners of the blanket, and without lifting the child off the floor, pull them around the perimeter of the room. The first team to finish a lap tells a sentence from the Bible story or repeats the memory verse, Mark 2:11.

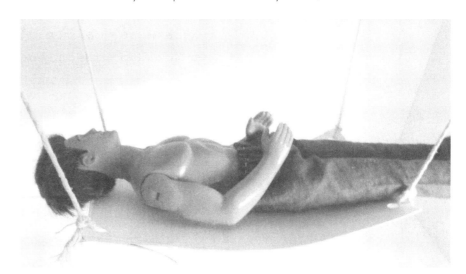

VOLUNTEER TIDBITS

Our children are surrounded by people wanting to speak lies into their lives. TV, music, peers, world events, and Satan all are pressing in to get a foothold. We need to faithfully rise above the noise and teach our children the Way, the Truth, and the Life. Proclaiming Jesus so they can receive, believe, and become children of God. Someone did it for us; we need to pass that gift on to them.

Turn to page 127 for more Volunteer Tidbits.

Object Lesson: Through the Roof

Materials

- Garden shovel

Say: What do we usually do with a tool like this? (*Children respond.*)

Usually we dig in the dirt or garden with a tool like this. In our Bible story today, some friends were doing some digging, but I don't think they had any shovels with them! Let's take a look. (*Read Mark 2:1–6.*)

Can you imagine digging through a roof with a garden tool? Today, we usually use shingles and nails on our roofs, but in Jesus' day, they did things a little differently. Usually, they would put wood beams across the top of the house and then layer sticks on top of the beams. Then, they would put a mixture of straw and mud to keep the rain out. This was a pretty complicated process and I don't think the homeowner would be very happy about the friends digging through his roof!

These friends knew that **God can heal**. They wanted to make sure their friend could get to Jesus, so they did something a little crazy! When they lowered their friend down to Jesus, he did heal the friend, but not in the way they were expecting.

What did Jesus say first to the man (Mark 2:5)? (*Children respond.*) Jesus healed the man of his sins! The friends were hoping that Jesus would heal their friend's body, but he did something even better. He saved the man from his sins.

God can heal our bodies and God can heal our hearts from sin. Of course, God is more powerful than any sickness, and to show how powerful he was, Jesus healed the paralyzed man's body, too. God is amazing. I'm so glad that **God can heal** our friends and he can heal us, too.

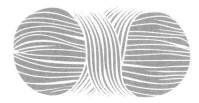

Materials
- Cardboard
- Craft sticks
- Yarn
- Poseable toy man

Easy Does It!

Say: It probably wasn't easy for the four friends to lower the paralyzed man down through that roof! Let's see how easy it is for you!

Directions: Have kids construct a mat for a toy man. Provide cardboard, craft sticks, yarn, and other materials you think might be helpful. Once the mat is constructed, have kids work in groups of four to try to lower the figure to the ground without having him slide off the mat.

Materials
- Construction paper
- Markers, pens, or pencils

Five Finger Prayer

Say: In today's lesson, the friends took the man to Jesus in order for him to be healed. Thankfully, we can talk to Jesus anytime through prayer. Let's make a craft to help us pray for others, remembering that **God can heal**.

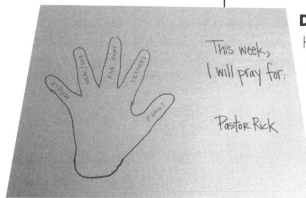

Directions: In this activity, kids use the fingers on their hands to remember to pray for people. Start by having kids trace their hand on a sheet of construction paper. In each finger, write groups of people as indicated: Thumb: Family and Friends; Pointer: Leaders (president, teachers, pastor, etc); Middle Finger: People Far Away; Ring Finger: Weak or Sick; Pinkie: Myself. Finish the craft by picking a specific person to pray for throughout the week.

Materials
- Teddy Graham crackers
- Frosting
- Plastic knives

Teddy Graham Snack

Say: Isn't it great that **God can heal**? Let's make a snack to remind us of today's lesson.

Directions: Provide graham crackers, frosting, and Teddy Graham crackers for the kids. Have them recreate the story with the edible figures.

Chapter 32: Zacchaeus

BIBLE STORY REFERENCE: Luke 19:1–10

MEMORY VERSE: *The Son of Man came to seek and to save the lost. Luke 19:10*

Big Idea
God Cares about Every Person

Overview

Say: Jesus spent a lot of time with people while he was on Earth. He wanted to tell them the good news about God and he wanted to show them how much he cared about them. Jesus helped people by healing them of sickness, getting rid of evil spirits, and teaching them all about the kingdom of God. **God cares about every person** and so did Jesus. Jesus even cared about the people that most people didn't like. One of those people was a man named Zacchaeus. (*Open with prayer requests, praises, and a time of prayer. Consider using the five-finger prayer from Chapter 31.*)

Bible Story

Say: What are some reasons people might not get along? What can make it difficult to like another person? (*Children respond.*)

The man in our Bible story today was not well liked. He was a tax collector and he often lied and cheated people to get extra money for himself. The Bible tells us that Zacchaeus wanted to see Jesus, but he couldn't get close because of the crowd. Let's read what he did in Luke 19:1–10. (*Read Scripture aloud.*) When Jesus went to Zacchaeus' house, the people were shocked because Zacchaeus was not a nice guy. This Bible story shows us that **God cares about every person,** even people who are difficult to get along with.

Outline
Overview
Bible Story
Opening Game
Object Lesson
Additional Optional Activities

Materials
- **Bibles**
- **Leaves or pictures of leaves**
- **Scratch Art papers**
  - **Stylus**
  - **Leaves**
  - **Glue**
- **Light blue construction paper**
- **2 buckets**
- **Masking tape**
- **Play gold coins**

Opening Game: Which Tree Is It?

Materials

- Leaves or pictures of leaves

Preparation: Gather some leaves or pictures of leaves before the game. Use library books or an online search to identify the leaves.

Say: In our Bible story, Zacchaeus climbed up a sycamore tree to get a better look at Jesus. In this game, I'm going to show you some leaves and you try to guess which tree they came from.

Directions: Hold up leaves, one at a time. Kids to shout out and try to guess what tree or plant the leaf came from.

VOLUNTEER TIDBITS

Encourage a staff person or volunteer to step outside their normal role and try something new that stretches them. Cross train each person on the team. This helps when people are unable to make their commitment.

Turn to page 131 for more helpful Volunteer Tidbits.

Object Lesson: Revealing Hidden Beauty

Materials

- Scratch Art papers, available online or at craft stores)
- Stylus

Directions: Hold up a sheet of Scratch Art paper. Be careful that there are no scratches in it yet.

Say: What do you see here? (*Children respond.*) **It's certainly not that impressive, is it? It just seems like a bunch of black. However, there is a little surprise to this paper. There's something hidden underneath.** (*Use the stylus to scratch off a bit of the black to reveal the rainbow colors underneath.*)

Say: Wow, I was not expecting that! I wonder if that is how the people felt about Zacchaeus. To them, he just looked like a bad guy. It was like his life was all black and filled with sin. But Jesus knew there was something else to Zacchaeus.

Jesus knew who God created Zacchaeus to be, and it wasn't a bad guy. God cares about every person, including the people who look like their lives are filled with nothing but sin. Zacchaeus had done a lot of bad, and people did not like him, but Jesus knew that Zacchaeus could change. And that's exactly what happened. (*Read Luke 19:8–9.*)

When Jesus came to Zacchaeus' house, Zacchaeus repented of his sins. We know that God forgives sins, and he forgave Zacchaeus. The Bible tells us that when we repent of our sins, God makes us into a whole new creation. (*Read 2 Corinthians 5:17.*) **God cares about every person** and he doesn't want us to keep living in our sin. He wants to turn our lives into something beautiful, just like this piece of scratch art!

Materials

- Leaves
- Glue
- Light blue construction paper

Tip: If using leaves from outside, kids may want to use tacky glue to hold them in place.

Materials

- 2 buckets
- Masking tape
- Play gold coins

Climb a Tree

Directions Head outside to visit the nearest tree and talk about what it might have been like for Zacchaeus to climb up the Sycamore in the midst of the crowds.

Say: Zacchaeus must have been pretty serious about seeing Jesus for him to climb up a tree. He could have looked silly or ripped his clothes trying to get into the branches. Zacchaeus really wanted to see Jesus and I'm sure he was glad to learn that **God cares about every person**!

Zach in a Tree

Say: Zacchaeus climbed a tree to see Jesus. Let's a make a tree like the one Zacchaeus may have climbed.

Directions: Hand each child a blank piece of construction paper. Using leaves from outside or cut out leaves, have them create a tree for Zacchaeus to climb.

Giving Back the Gold

Preparation: Against opposite walls, place a bucket. Use masking tape to make a line dividing the playing area between the two walls.

Say: After Zacchaeus spent time with Jesus, he realized that he was wrong to trick people out of their money. He gave the money back. In this game, we're going to try to get rid of some gold coins, too!

Directions: Divide kids up into two groups and set the timer for five minutes. Scatter gold coins all over the floor. Kids must pick up a coin from their side of the playing field (one at a time), run to the opposite team's bucket and drop it in. If a kid is tagged when on the opposite team's side, they must drop the coin and return to their own side to try again. The team who has the LEAST amount of gold coins in their bucket when the timer beeps tells a sentence about the Bible story.

# Chapter 33: Jesus Feeds 5,000 People

BIBLE STORY REFERENCE: Matthew 14:13–21, John 6:5–13

MEMORY VERSE: *Jesus then took the loaves, gave thanks, and distributed to those who were seated as much as they wanted. He did the same with the fish. John 6:11*

Big Idea
God Provides

Overview

Say: Jesus did amazing things when he was on Earth. People came to him from all over the land and followed him to see his many miracles. Jesus spent a lot of time teaching the people about God and about God's kingdom. One day, Jesus was teaching the people and healing the sick. There was a huge crowd that had gathered and Jesus' disciples were concerned that the people would need to eat soon. They wanted to send the people away, but Jesus had other plans. *(Open with prayer requests, praises, and a time of prayer.)*

Bible Story

Say: In today's Bible story, a big crowd gathered to hear from Jesus. When it came time to eat, the disciples could only find one boy with a very small lunch to share. Let's read what happened in John 6:5–13. Not only was there enough for everyone in the crowd (over 5,000 people!), there were even twelve baskets of leftovers. That is a miracle! **God provides,** but it's not always in the ways we are expecting. I am glad that God is powerful and that he can provide for you and me.

Outline
Overview
Bible Story
Opening Game
Object Lesson
Additional Optional Activities

Materials
- **Bibles**
- **Bonus Activity: Reproducible pages 237–238**
- **Popcorn popper**
- **½ cup popcorn**
- **Butter**
- **Large bowl**
- **Napkins**
- **Dinner rolls**
- **Butter**
- **Jam**
- **Plastic knives**
- **Small bucket**
- **Sponges or pool noodles**
- **Lacing material or embroidery floss**
- **Fish beads**
- **Pony beads**

Opening Game: Favorite Foods

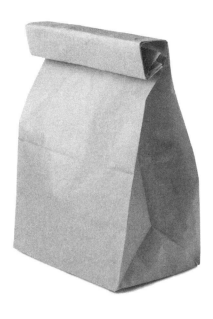

Say: How many of you usually pack a lunch? What is your favorite thing to get in your lunch? (*Children respond.*) **We're not sure if fish and bread were the boy in our Bible story's favorite foods, but we're going to pretend they were. In this game, we're going to try and remember everyone's favorite food.**

Directions: Kids sit in a circle, facing each other. Start with the child on your right. Have them say their name and their favorite food. The next child in line (to the right) repeats the first child's name and favorite food. Then, they add their own name and favorite food to the list. This continues around the circle, with each child trying to remember all the names and favorite foods that came before him. If it gets too difficult, allow the kids to help each other remember.

VOLUNTEER TIDBITS

Preparation

- Pray during the week for the lesson, the team, and the children.
- Read the story in the Bible—helps you gather additional facts and possibly some sensory ideas.
- Memorize the story ahead of time. You don't have to tell it perfectly, word for word from the book.
- Arrive at least fifteen minutes early for class.
- Have all the materials ready to go before the children arrive.
- Pray together as a team.
- Make sure all volunteers know what the key point is and what they are going to help with in class.

Turn to page 135 for more helpful Volunteer Tidbits.

Object Lesson: Popping Out of Control

Materials

- Popcorn popper
- ½ cup popcorn
- Butter, melted
- Large bowl
- Napkins

Say: (*Hold up the popcorn kernels.*) **Does this seem like a good lunch to you? Does it seem like it would be enough for everyone in our group?** (*Children respond.*)

It doesn't seem like that much to me! Even if I ate all these kernels myself, I think I would still be hungry. But an amazing thing happens when I put these kernels inside the popper.

Directions: Put the popcorn kernels inside the popcorn popper and turn it on. Be sure to have the large bowl under the blower to catch the falling popcorn. It might take one or two minutes for the kernels to begin popping.

Say: Wow! That's amazing how those tiny kernels transformed into a whole bowlful of popcorn! Now there's enough for everyone in the group. (*Pour on the melted butter and serve the popcorn to the kids.*)

Say: The popcorn popping wasn't a miracle, but it was pretty cool. In our Bible story today, though, Jesus did perform a miracle when he fed all those people with just a small amount of food. (*Read Matthew 14:18–21.*) **God provides** in amazing and unexpected ways sometimes. **God provides** even when it doesn't make sense. **God provides** because he is powerful. I have seen **God provide** in my own life and I hope you have seen it in yours, too!

Directions: Kids tell about times that God has provided in their lives as you finish eating the popcorn.

Materials

- Dinner rolls
- Butter
- Jam
- Plastic knives
- Napkins

Materials

- Small bucket, one for each child or team
- Sponges or pool noodles

Materials

- Lacing material or embroidery floss
- Fish beads, two for each child
- Pony beads, five for each child

Bonus Idea: Children tie knots between the beads to add interest.

Little Loaves

Say: There's something extra delicious about fresh baked bread. In our Bible story, the boy had five loaves of bread that were probably about the size of dinner rolls. Let's enjoy these rolls, remembering that **God provides**.

Directions: Pass out a dinner roll to each child. Children top with butter and/or jam and enjoy as a snack.

Gather Up the Leftovers

Say: Not only did Jesus provide enough food for everyone in the crowd, but there were twelve baskets of leftovers as well! That's even more than Thanksgiving! Isn't it great to know that God often provides above and beyond our needs?

Directions: In this game, kids will use small buckets (one bucket for each child or have them work in teams) to gather up "leftovers" from around the room. Cut up pieces of car sponges or pool noodles to represent the leftover food. Set the timer for one minute and let them run! Player or team who has the most "food" in their bucket at the end recites, or chooses a volunteer to recite, the memory verse.

Fish and Loaves Bracelet

Directions: Have kids make bracelets using fish beads and pony beads (available online or in craft stores) to represent the loaves and fish from today's Bible story.

Say: This bracelet will help us remember that **God provides**. Use these bracelets to remember that God is with you when you have a challenge and will provide for you. Use them to share the day's story with your friends and family.

Turn to page 237–238 for a Bonus Activity.

Chapter 34: Jesus Calms the Storm

BIBLE STORY REFERENCE: Mark 4:37–41

MEMORY VERSE: *The men were amazed and asked, "What kind of man is this? Even the winds and the waves obey him!" Matthew 8:27*

Big Idea
Jesus Is Powerful

Overview

Say: Jesus was no ordinary man. **Jesus was powerful.** He was more powerful than sickness. He could heal people. He could feed many people in a miraculous way. Jesus was a man, but he was also God. **Jesus is still powerful today!** Jesus is more powerful than nature. He can control all things. *(Open with prayer requests, praises, and a time of prayer.)*

Bible Story

Say: Some people love to watch thunderstorms, especially when they are safe inside a warm house. In our Bible story, the disciples were in a thunderstorm, but they didn't have much shelter! They were on the open sea. They were afraid they were going to drown. Let's turn in our Bibles to Mark 4:37–41. *(Read Scripture aloud.)*

The disciples must have forgotten that Jesus is powerful. Jesus spoke to the wind and waves and they immediately stopped. I'm so glad that Jesus can control all things.

Outline
Overview
Bible Story
Opening Game
Object Lesson
Additional Optional Activities

Materials
- Bibles
- Bonus Activity: Reproducible page 239
- Squirt bottles
- Water
- Plastic toy boats
- Plastic tarps
- Banana
- Toothpick or needle
- Glue
- Small plastic water bottles
- Glitter
- Duct tape
- Torn strips of blue construction paper
- Black construction paper
- Brown construction paper
- Glue
- Markers
- Toy people
- Video camera or cell phone

Opening Game: What a Storm!

Materials

- Squirt bottles
- Water
- Plastic toy boats, available at most dollar stores
- Plastic tarps

Tip: Do this activity outside if you can.

Directions: Fill bottles with water. Set up plastic toy boats along one edge of a table. Protect furniture and/or carpet with plastic tarps.

Say: The storm in our Bible story today was so bad that the disciples thought they might drown. In our game, we're going to hit these little boats with some serious rain power, too.

Directions: For each boat, give one child a spray bottle full of water. At the start of the race, kids will spray (have the setting on a straight stream) their boats with water, trying to get them to move across the table. The player whose boat is the first to fall off the table tells, or chooses a volunteer to tell, a sentence about the Bible story.

VOLUNTEER TIDBITS

ABCs of Salvation

- **Admit** you are a sinner (Romans 3:23).
- **Believe** in Jesus as your Savior and receive him (John 3:16).
- **Confess** that Jesus is Lord and choose to follow him (Romans 10:9).

Tip: Watch for situations where kids feel obligated to pray with a group. This leads to following instead of deciding.

Turn to page 139 for more Volunteer Tips.

Object Lesson: Magic Slicing Banana

Materials

- Banana
- Toothpick or needle

Preparation: Use the toothpick or needle to poke a hole in one side of the banana.* Move the toothpick or needle back and forth while inside the peel to slice the fruit. Remove the toothpick or needle and move it a few inches down the banana. Repeat the process to slice the fruit again. Do it a third time, keeping track of where your slices are.

Say: Hello everyone! Today I'm going to do something pretty powerful. I'm going to slice this banana without even peeling it. Who thinks I can do this powerful task? (*Children respond.*)

Directions: Place the banana on the table with the holes from the toothpick or needle facing down, so the kids cannot see them. Pretend to karate chop the banana in approximately the same places where you pre-sliced the fruit.

Say: There! Now, inside this banana, the fruit is sliced. Do you believe it? (*Open banana to reveal the sliced-up fruit.*)

Now, this was just an illusion. I'm not really that powerful. But there is someone who is that powerful: **Jesus is powerful**. He stopped a storm with a single command. (*Read Mark 4:35–41.*) Jesus can do amazing things and I'm so glad he is in control.

> *** Note:** To see a video on how to prepare the banana, do an online search for "sliced banana illusion."

Materials

- Glue
- Water
- Small plastic water bottles, one for each child
- Glitter
- Duct tape

Optional

- Food coloring

Materials

- Torn strips of blue construction paper
- Black construction paper, one sheet for each child
- Brown construction paper
- Glue

Bonus Idea: For added dimension, kids paint the blue paper before tearing it.

Materials

- Toy people
- Video camera or cell phone

Tip: Search online for "Galilee boat playset" to find a great set of toy people.

Alternate Idea: Kids create a stop-motion video based on today's Bible story.

Calm Down Bottle

Preparation: Make a mixture of twenty-percent glue and eighty-percent water. Pour mixture into small plastic water bottles and secure lids. Prepare one bottle for each child.

Say: Today we learned that **Jesus is powerful.** He can calm a storm by just speaking. Let's make a project to remind us of Jesus' calming power.

Directions: Children add glitter to bottles. Optional: Children add a drop or two of food coloring. Assist children to secure the lids and duct tape the bottle to assure it doesn't come open.

Have each child find a quiet spot in the room. Instruct them to shake the bottle, and then pray as they watch the glitter slowly settle to the bottom again.

Torn Paper Ocean

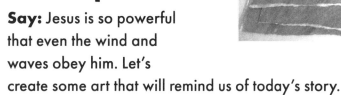

Say: Jesus is so powerful that even the wind and waves obey him. Let's create some art that will remind us of today's story.

Directions: Use torn strips of paper to create ocean waves. Begin with a black piece of construction paper for the base. Tear a blue piece of construction paper horizontally. Glue the blue pieces onto the black sheet to create ocean waves. Add a brown construction paper boat if desired.

Stop Motion Video

Say: What an adventure it must have been to be with Jesus on that boat. Let's create a video together of the Bible story.

Directions: Video children using toy figures to reenact the Bible story in their own words.

Turn to page 239 for a Bonus Activity.

Chapter 35: Mary and Martha

BIBLE STORY REFERENCE: Luke 10:38–42

MEMORY VERSE: *Mary has chosen what is better, and it will not be taken away from her. Luke 10:42*

**Big Idea
God Wants Us
to Spend Time
with Him**

Overview

Say: Jesus spent a lot of time with people while he was on Earth. Besides his disciples, Jesus had some special friends that he liked to visit and spend time with. Some of these friends were Mary, Martha, and Lazarus. (*Open with prayer requests, praises, and a time of prayer.*)

Bible Story

Say: What kind of chores do you have to do? (*Children respond.*) Usually everyone in the family has some kind of responsibilities or chores, such as cleaning our rooms or helping with dinner. When a guest comes, there are even more responsibilities.

One day, when Jesus was visiting, his friend Martha got upset. She was busy trying to get dinner ready for her guests, and her sister Mary was not helping at all! Let's read what happened in Luke 10:38–42. (*Read Scripture aloud.*)

Martha wanted things to be just right for Jesus' visit, but she was so busy preparing that she forgot to spend any time with him! **God wants us to spend time with him,** but sometimes we get distracted with other "good things" and we forget just like Martha did.

Outline
Overview
Bible Story
Opening Game
Object Lesson
Additional Optional Activities

Materials
- Bibles
- Reproducible page 240
- Plastic utensils
- Paper plates
- Cooking supplies
- Post-It Notes
- Pencils or markers
- Children's worship music or recorded Bible story and player
- 12x12-inch fabric squares
- Glue
- Fiberfill

Opening Game: Coming to Dinner

Materials
- Reproducible page 240
- Plastic utensils
- Paper plates

Optional: Add cups, napkins, bowls, and/or placemats.

Preparation: Copy page 240, making one for each team of three to five players. Place at one end of the playing area. Place the plastic utensils, paper plates, and any other supplies at the other end of the playing area.

Say: In our Bible story, Martha was getting a visitor! Jesus was coming to Martha's house to spend some time with her and her family. In this game, we're going to pretend to set the table and get ready for Jesus' arrival.

Directions: Divide kids up into teams. When the race begins, the first child on each team will grab one piece, race to the template and begin "setting the table." They will race back, tag the next person in line, who will then continue the process with another piece. As each team completes the template or place setting, they tell a sentence about the Bible story or recite the memory verse.

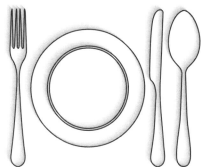

VOLUNTEER TIDBITS
Teaching Tips
- Use your Bible. Read the story from your Bible.
- Use your curriculum book.
- Ask staff or experienced teachers for ideas.
- Get supplies from the resource room.
- Research ideas from the Internet.
- Stretch your imagination!

Turn to page 143 for more Volunteer Tidbits.

Object Lesson: Cooking for Jesus

Materials

• Cooking supplies (pots, pans, spoons, spices, etc)

Say: Does anyone here like to cook? What is your favorite thing to prepare? (*Children respond.*)

Directions: Kids examine your cooking supplies. Encourage conversation, asking whether or not they have ever used each tool before.

Say: Cooking can be a lot of fun, especially when we are preparing a special dish for guests. Sometimes though, it seems like we spend so much time in the kitchen getting dinner ready that we don't have any time to actually spend with our guests! That's exactly what happened to Martha from our Bible story today. (*Read Luke 10:38–42.*)

I wonder if Martha was surprised by Jesus' response. I sure was! It wasn't wrong for Martha to be doing all that cooking, but she had forgotten the most important thing.

Mary knew that Jesus was a special person and she wanted to spend her time listening and learning from him. **God wants us to spend time with him** and sometimes that means that we have to say no to other things in our lives. That doesn't mean that those things are bad. But we only have so much time every day and the most important thing we can do is spending time with God.

(*Discuss things that might get in the way of spending time with God.*)
How can we make sure that we spend time with God every day?

Additional Optional Activities

Materials
- Post-It Notes
- Pencils or markers

Prayer Wall

Say: One way we can spend time with God is through prayer. Let's write requests and praises on these sticky notes and then spend some time praying about them.

Directions: Kids write or draw things they are thankful for on the Post-It Notes. Encourage them to write requests about leaders, people who are sick, people who are traveling, or people who are feeling sad. Place the sticky notes on a wall to create a prayer station.

Materials
- Children's worship music or recorded Bible story and player

Optional
- Headphones

Listening Station

Say: We can spend time with God through prayer, through reading or listening to the Bible, and through singing.

Directions: Set up a cozy corner in the room for kids to spend some time listening to children's worship music or recorded Bible stories. Optional: Children use headphones.

Materials
- 12x12-inch fabric squares, two for each child
- Glue
- Fiberfill

Bonus Idea: Give children fabric paint to decorate their pillow. Be aware of drying time and the need to transport it home.

Puffy Pillow

Say: Mary might have used some kind of pillow or floor cushion to sit on as she listened to Jesus. Let's create our own pillow to remind us to spend time with God.

Directions: Give each child two fabric squares. Carefully, help kids hot glue (or fabric glue) three sides of the pillow together. Glue the fourth side, leaving a small hole for turning pillow case inside out. Once the glue is set, flip the fabric right side out and stuff with fiberfill. Carefully glue opening shut to create a finished pillow.

Chapter 36: Lazarus

BIBLE STORY REFERENCE: John 11:17–44

MEMORY VERSE: *Jesus said to her, "I am the resurrection and the life. The one who believes in me will live, even though they die. John 11:25*

Big Idea
Jesus Is More Powerful Than Death

Overview

Say: Jesus was good friends with Mary, Martha, and Lazarus. He often spent time at their house, visiting with them. One day, Jesus heard that Lazarus was sick, but he did not go to him right away. It didn't seem to make any sense, but Jesus did it so that God would be glorified. *(Open with prayer requests, praises, and a time of prayer. Consider using the Post-it Note prayer wall from Chapter 35.)*

Bible Story

Say: Jesus was no ordinary man. He could do incredible things. Not only did he spend his entire life without sinning, he also performed many miracles.

One day, Jesus' friend Lazarus was sick so his sisters sent a message to Jesus. Mary and Martha probably expected Jesus to come right away when he learned that Lazarus was sick, but Jesus surprised everyone when he waited to visit. Let's read what happened in John 11:17–27. *(Read Scripture aloud.)*

By the time Jesus made it to his friends' home, Lazarus was already dead. It seems like this would be the end of the story, but **Jesus is more powerful than death**. Let's continue reading in John 11:38–44. *(Read Scripture aloud.)* Wow! Jesus allowed Lazarus to die because he wanted the people to see how powerful he truly was.

Outline
Overview
Bible Story
Opening Game
Object Lesson
Additional Optional Activities

Materials
- Bibles
- Blindfold
- Plastic water bottle
- Pre-stretched balloon
- 1 packet yeast
- 1 teaspoon sugar
- Permanent marker
- Several rolls of toilet paper
- Paper
- Pencils
- Notecards or sheets of cardstock
- Paper plates
- Grey paint
- Construction paper

Opening Game: Jesus, Where Are You?

Materials
- Blindfold

Say: It must have been hard for Mary and Martha while they waited for Jesus to arrive. We're going to play a game that involves some slow moving and some waiting as well.

Directions: The game is played like Red Light, Green Light, but "It" cannot see the other players. Kids line up on one side of the room. Assign a volunteer to be "It." "It" stands on the opposite side of the playing area, blindfolded. Children move toward "It," according to the directions called by "It":

Green light: kids walk fast

Yellow light: kids walk in slow motion

Red light: kids stop

The first child to reach "It" gets to call out directions for the next round.

VOLUNTEER TIDBITS
Resources for Volunteers
- Your Bible—Read the story from your Bible
- Use your curriculum book
- Ask staff or experienced teachers for ideas
- Resource room
- Internet
- Your imagination

Turn to page 147 for more Volunteer Tidbits.

Object Lesson: Remarkable Risen Balloon

Materials

- Plastic water bottle, 16-ounce or smaller
- Pre-stretched balloon
- 1 packet yeast
- 1 teaspoon sugar
- Permanent marker

Optional

- Funnel

* Note: The balloon takes about twenty minutes before it begins to inflate. This waiting fits in great with the rest of the story. Try to time the lesson so that the balloon begins to inflate at the appropriate part of the lesson, or have a duplicate started ahead time hiding to pull out at the last minute.

Preparation: Begin by filling the water bottle with about an inch of warm water. Add the yeast and swirl to mix. Add the sugar and swirl to mix. Blow up the balloon a few times to stretch it. Show kids the balloon.

Say: Let's imagine this is Lazarus. (*Blow balloon up a little and draw a face on it with the marker.*) **Right now, Lazarus is feeling pretty good. But as we read in our Bible story, Lazarus got sick. Mary and Martha sent a message to Jesus, but it didn't seem like Jesus was coming. Lazarus got even sicker.** (*Let some air out of the balloon.*) **He felt worse and worse.** (*Deflate the balloon till it is almost empty.*) **Pretty soon, Lazarus was dead.** (*Let all the air out of the balloon.*)

Mary and Martha were so upset. They buried Lazarus in a tomb and spent several days crying and mourning. (*Put balloon over opening of bottle and set to the side a bit. **) **People came from nearby towns to mourn with Mary and Martha and to try and comfort them.** (*Read Matthew 11:18.*)

Finally, Jesus arrived. Martha ran out to meet him. (*Read Matthew 11:20–27.*) **Do you think Martha was surprised by Jesus' answer?** (*Allow kids to respond.*)

I wonder if Martha was beginning to understand that Jesus is more powerful than death. After Jesus talked to both Mary and Martha, he asked that the stone be rolled away from Lazarus' tomb. (*Read Matthew 11:38–44.*)

At first, the people didn't want to obey Jesus! They thought that it would be too stinky to roll away that stone. They didn't realize that Jesus is more powerful than death. When Jesus spoke to Lazarus, an amazing thing happened (*bring the bottle back in front of the kids and swirl it a bit*)— **Lazarus rose from the dead! Just like this balloon reinflated, Lazarus came back to life. Jesus is truly amazing!**

Materials
- Several rolls of toilet paper

Wrapping Up Lazarus Game

Say: Just like Lazarus was wrapped in grave clothes, let's wrap a friend from head to toe in toilet paper.

Directions: Kids must work as a team to wrap one person up as completely as they can in toilet paper. Start by setting the timer for four or five minutes. Give each team (three or four kids works best) a few rolls of toilet paper and let them go wild. The object of the game is to have one person as covered as possible when the timer beeps.

Materials
- Paper
- Pencils
- Notecards or sheets of cardstock

Jesus Will Comfort You

Directions: In this activity, kids will use a concordance to find the word "comfort" in the Bible. Encourage them to write meaningful verses on notecards and perhaps share the verses with others who need to be comforted.

Say: Even though Jesus knew that he was about to raise Lazarus from the dead, he still mourned with the family. Jesus provides comfort to us when we are sad. He knows just how we feel because he has felt the same way.

Materials
- Paper plates
- Grey paint
- Construction paper

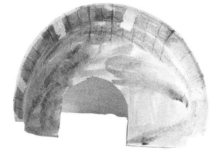

Paper-Plate Tomb

Directions: Use a paper plate to create a tomb for Lazarus. Use a grey or paper plate (or paint a white one), and cut the paper plate in half. Cut a small opening in one paper plate half. Glue or staple the halves together to form a small tomb. If desired, use cardstock or crinkled construction paper to make a stone to place in front of the opening.

Say: Lazarus was in the tomb for four days by the time Jesus arrived. People thought there was no hope left, but they soon learned that **Jesus is more powerful than death.**

Chapter 37: The Good Samaritan

**Big Idea
God Wants
Us to Help
Others**

BIBLE STORY REFERENCE: Luke 10:25–37

MEMORY VERSE: *Love your neighbor as yourself.* Luke 10:27

Overview

Say: Jesus helped many people while he was on Earth.
People were often surprised by the people he helped and
the people he chose to hang out with. Jesus loved everyone,
even if they had not lived a good life. He loved them even
if they were from a bad part of town. He showed kindness
to everyone because **God wants us to help others.**
(*Open with prayer requests, praises, and a time of prayer.*)

Bible Story

Say: Do you ever do anything to show love
to your neighbors? (*Children respond.*)

In today's Bible story, a teacher of the law wanted to know who
his neighbor was. The man knew, according to the law, that he
should love his neighbor, but he wasn't sure who exactly that
meant. Jesus surprised the man with a strange answer. Jesus
told a parable about a Samaritan, a people group that the
Jews did not like. Let's turn in our Bibles to Luke 10:30–35.
(*Read Scripture aloud.*) Through Jesus' parable, we learn that
everyone we come in contact with is a neighbor, even if it's a
person we wouldn't normally get along with. **God wants us
to help others,** including people who are different from us.

Outline
**Overview
Bible Story
Opening Game
Object Lesson
Additional Optional Activities**

Materials
- **Bibles**
- **Reproducible page 241**
- **Team jersey**
- **Rival team jersey**
- **Markers or crayons**
- **Stickers**
- **Kindness video**

Opening Game: Donkey Ride

Say: In our Bible story, a Jewish man was robbed and beaten up as he walked along the road. A passing Samaritan put the injured man on his donkey and took him to a local inn to allow him to rest and recover. In this game, we're going to give some donkey rides just like the Samaritan did.

Directions: Kids divide into teams of four. One child will be the Samaritan and one will be the beaten Jewish man. The other two will serve as the donkey.

Donkey kids get on their hands and knees as the beaten man lays across both their backs. The beat-up man must lay flat, he cannot move or hold on to keep himself on the "donkey." The Samaritan can guide the donkey and help to keep the beaten man balanced. Teams race to touch a wall on the opposite side of the playing area. The first team to touch the wall repeats the Memory Verse, Luke 10:27.

VOLUNTEER TIDBITS

There are approximately 936 weeks from when a child is born to when they graduate high school. Children in the average Children's ministry (Birth through the finish of elementary) travel through about 536 of those weeks. Each year you will have them fifty-two weeks for one or two hours a week. The average child misses one-third of those weeks. That takes it down to about thirty-eight weeks to impact them. If you teach for about twenty minutes a session, you do the math. That is very little time in a year. That is why incorporating learning and message reinforcement in games and activities throughout their time with you is vital. It extends the learning.

Turn to page 151 for more Volunteer Tidbits.

Object Lesson: Helping a Rival

Materials

- Team jersey
- Rival team jersey

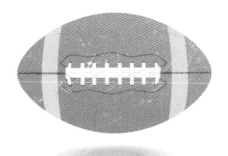

Say: How many of you like sports? Do you watch with the family? What team do you cheer for? (*Children respond.*) I'm a pretty big fan of football, too. In fact, I have a story to tell you, and I need two volunteers to do it.

Select two volunteers and have them wear the team jerseys. In our neck of the woods, we cheer for the Steelers, so I'll be using Steelers and Browns in the story. Please replace with whatever teams are appropriate for your region or town. Read the following story and encourage kids in jerseys to act along:

A Steelers fan was walking along the road when a couple of thugs beat him up, took all his money, and left him almost dead. A pastor walked by, but did not help. Another worker in the church went by, but also did not help. Then, a Cleveland Browns fan came down the road. Do you think he helped? (*Children respond.*)

Surprisingly, he did! Not only did he help the Steelers fan up, he took him to a nearby hotel and ordered him room service. He also left his credit card number in case the Steelers fan needed anything else.

What do you think of the Cleveland Browns fan? (*Children respond.*) His actions were pretty surprising. Even though these two fans are usually enemies, the Browns fan still showed kindness. That reminds me a lot of our Bible story today. (*Read Luke 10:30–37.*) Usually Jews and Samaritans were enemies, but the Samaritan was a true neighbor to the man who needed help. Just like the Samaritan, God wants us to help others.

Service Project

Say: In our Bible story, the Samaritan just happened upon a man who needed help. Sometimes that happens for us too, but not always. Let's think about ways that we can be a neighbor to people in our community.

Directions: Plan a service project with the kids (search online for "Service projects for kids" if you need help with ideas).

Get-Well Cards

Preparation: Copy page 241, making one for each child.

Say: Do you know someone who is sick or recovering from injury right now? A simple card can do a lot to encourage them and bring some cheer. Let's make some cards together.

Directions: Kids color cards, write greetings and give cards to a person in need.

Materials

- Reproducible page 241
- Markers or crayons
- Stickers

Materials

- Kindness video

Kindness. Pass It On.

Say: There are many ways we can help others. Let's watch this video and look for ways in our daily lives that we can show love to others.

Directions: There are several powerful videos available online (search: kindness, pass it on) that the kids might enjoy watching. Seeing kindness in action might be inspirational to them as they see how it changes someone's day. Search for a video that fits your group and show it to remind them that **God wants us to help others**.

Chapter 38: Lost Things

BIBLE STORY REFERENCE: Luke 15:3–24

MEMORY VERSE: *In the same way, I tell you, there is rejoicing in the presence of the angels of God over one sinner who repents."* Luke 15:10

**Big Idea
Every Person
Is Important
to God**

Overview

Say: Jesus loved spending time with people while he lived on Earth. Sometimes the teachers of the law thought Jesus was hanging around the wrong type of people. Jesus wanted them to see that **every person is important to God**, so he told some stories about some lost things. (*Open with prayer requests, praises, and a time of prayer.*)

Bible Story

Say: Have you ever lost anything? How did you feel? How did you feel if you found it? (*Children respond.*)

It's never fun to lose something—especially if it's something important. In our Bible story today, there are three things that are lost: a lost sheep, a lost coin, and a lost son.

Let's read about the lost sheep in Luke 15:3–7. (*Read Scripture aloud.*) It might not seem like one sheep is important, but it was! In the same way, **every person is important to God**. When the shepherd found the lost sheep, he called all his friends and celebrated.

The same thing happened when the woman found her lost coin (Luke 15:8–9) and when a lost son returned to his father (Luke 15:21–24). In the same way, God celebrates anytime someone becomes a Christian because every person is important to God.

Outline
**Overview
Bible Story
Opening Game
Object Lesson
Additional Optional Activities**

Materials
- Bibles
- Reproducible page 242
- Play gold coins
- Lost and found box
- "Junk" items
- Markers
- White construction paper
- Scissors
- Glue
- Gray and blue cardstock
- Black felt
- White buttons

Opening Game: Lost Coin

Materials

- Play gold coins

Preparation: Hide coins around the room before the kids arrive. Make sure there is at least one coin for each child.

Say: When the woman in our Bible story lost a coin, she stopped everything else to look for the coin and she didn't stop until she found it. In the same way, every person is important to God. In this game, I've hidden some coins around the room. We're going to pretend these are lost coins. Go search for one lost coin and when you've found it, give a shout (celebrate!) and return to the group.

VOLUNTEER TIDBITS
Teen Training

- Be daily in God's Word.
- What are your talents? What do you really enjoy doing?
- Pray for the children and tell them you did.
- Know what is being taught each week and what your role is.
- Try a new role.

Turn to page 155 for more Volunteer Tidbits.

Object Lesson: Lost and Found

Materials
- Lost and found box

Say: What can you tell me about this box? This is a lost and found box. It's filled with stuff that people left behind. You might think that these things aren't important because they were forgotten, but chances are, someone is probably really missing the stuff inside this box. (*Take a few things out of the box, discussing with the kids who might have owned it.*)

After awhile, if no one comes to claim this stuff, it will be given away or thrown away. But that's not how it works with God. He doesn't want anyone who is lost, or not in a relationship with him, to stay that way. **Every person is important to God**. He wants to have a relationship with every person.

God is always working in your life to bring you closer to him. Sometimes God brings you a friend who tells you about Jesus. Sometimes God has a neighbor invite you to church. Sometimes God gives you a relative who loves Jesus and shows you how great that relationship is. No matter how God does it, he comes looking for you—just like that shepherd in our story. **Every person is important to God**.

If you don't have a friendship with God, this lesson might be just the thing God is using to help you stop being lost. Don't wait another day! Every person is important to God, including you. If you want to start a friendship with God, let's pray about it today.

Directions: Allow some time for kids to think about this decision and ask if anyone would like to begin a friendship with God today. Pray with them using simple language, asking God to forgive their sins and be friends with them forever.

Materials

- "Junk" items (cardboard boxes and tubes, aluminum foil, buttons, wooden dowels, yarn, recyclables, lids, dairy containers, paper plates, old socks, etc.)

Bonus Idea: Challenge children to work in teams.

Materials

- Markers
- White construction paper
- Scissors
- Glue
- Gray and blue cardstock
- Black felt
- White buttons

Materials

- Reproducible page 242

Junk Robot

Say: Some people might think this stuff isn't important, but look at the amazing things we are able to create with it!

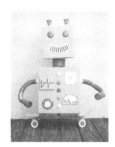

Directions: Bring in some "junk" or "lost things" for the kids to create and explore with. Encourage them to build a robot or some other creation.

Lost Sheep

Say: Just like one lost sheep was important to that shepherd, **every person is important to God.** Let's make a craft to remind us of today's Bible story.

Directions: Kids use marker to draw a cloud-like shape in the middle of a sheet of white paper for the sheep's body. Children cut out the cloud shape and glue to a sheet of gray or blue cardstock. Next, children cut the felt pieces to make four legs and a head and glue the legs at the bottom of the body and the head to the side of the body. Glue buttons inside the cloud shape and to the head to form eyes.

Lost Things Maze

Preparation: Copy page 242, making one for each child.

Say: Just like the shepherd looked for his lost sheep, so does Jesus continue to seek out people who don't know him. When we don't know Jesus we are really lost. Let's help the shepherd find his sheep.

Directions: Children use their fingers to trace the lines to help the shepherd find the sheep.

Chapter 39: Parable of the Seeds and Soil

BIBLE STORY REFERENCE: Matthew 13:3–23

MEMORY VERSE: *The seed falling on good soil refers to someone who hears the word and understands it. Matthew 13:23*

**Big Idea
God Wants Us
to Listen to and
Obey the Bible**

Overview

Say: Jesus told many different types of stories. Sometimes he explained the stories, and sometimes he did not. One day, Jesus told his disciples a parable (story) about some seeds and soil. After the crowds left, Jesus explained what the story meant to his disciples. (*Open with prayer requests, praises, and a time of prayer.*)

Bible Story

Say: When we plant seeds, we can't just throw them in the ground and walk away! Just like in our story today, many things could happen to the seeds that would keep them from growing properly. Let's read what happened to the seeds in today's Bible story by turning to Matthew 13:3–8. (*Read Scripture aloud.*)

The disciples were confused about what the parable meant, so they asked Jesus to explain it to them. Let's read what Jesus said in Matthew 13:18–23. (*Read Scripture aloud.*)

There are many things that can get in the way of us obeying the Bible, but **God wants us to listen to and obey the Bible.** Sometimes it is hard to do, but listening to the Bible and working to understand it will change our lives and help us to live the way God wants us to.

Outline
Overview
Bible Story
Opening Game
Object Lesson
Additional Optional Activities

Materials
- Bibles
- Cotton balls
- Bucket
- Clothespins
- Stopwatch
- Thriving plant
- Withered plant
- Seeds
- Soil
- Small pots or plastic cups
- Pumpkin seeds
- Food color
- Plastic bags
- Newspaper
- Plastic bags
- Construction paper
- Glue

Opening Game: Bird Snatch

Materials

- Cotton balls
- Bucket
- Clothespins, one for each child
- Stopwatch

Preparation: Scatter cotton balls around the room. Place the bucket in the middle of the room.

Say: In our Bible story, a man threw seeds onto the ground. The first set of seeds didn't even stand a chance because they were snatched away by birds. In this game, you will pretend to be the birds. Grab the seeds scattered around the room and put them in the bucket.

Directions: Give each child a clothespin to use like a beak to pick up the cotton-ball "seeds." Players may only pick up one "seed" at a time.

On your signal, children pick up the "seeds" one at a time and put them in the bucket. Time how long it takes children. Play another round, challenging children to beat their time from the first round.

VOLUNTEER TIDBITS

There are many things to champion in our world; disease cures, baby seals, political activism, hunger, homelessness, the list goes on and on. This year you have endeavored to give your time to change the spiritual path of a child. That single decision and life-changing commitment has not only impacted that child, but everyone that child will impact. You chose to serve in a ministry that helps children receive, believe, and become part of God's family.

Turn to page 159 for more Volunteer Tidbits.

Object Lesson: Seeds, Soils, and Plants

Materials

- Thriving plant
- Withered plant

Say: Have you ever grown a plant? What kind of things are needed to keep a plant healthy and strong? (*Children respond.*)

Jesus told a story about some seeds and some soil. A farmer threw some seeds on the ground, but not all of them landed in the right place. Let's take a look. (*Read Matthew 13:3–8. Show kids the withered plant.*) **What kind of seed and soil does this remind you of?**

This plant reminds me of the rocky and shallow soil. The plant did not have a chance to develop good roots. If a plant doesn't have good roots, it can't get enough water and pretty soon, it dries up and dies. The Bible tells us that this happens to people, in a way, too.

God wants us to listen to and obey the Bible, but that doesn't always happen. This withered plant is like someone who hears the Bible and is very excited about it. But they don't take the time to develop roots. They don't keep reading the Bible. They let other things become more important than spending time with God. Pretty soon, they start to dry out spiritually. They look like this plant. But that's not God's desire for our lives. **God wants us to listen to and obey the Bible**.

(*Show the kids the thriving plant.*) **What kind of seed and soil does this remind you of?** (*Children respond.*) **This plant reminds me of the last kind of soil. It was good soil. A person who is this kind of soil listens to and obeys the Bible. They make sure to spend time with God by reading the Bible and praying. They try to obey God's commands and they grow spiritually. They are like a healthy and strong plant.

Materials

- Seeds
- Soil
- Small pots or plastic cups

Materials

- Pumpkin seeds
- Food color
- Newspaper
- Plastic bags, one for each child
- Construction paper
- Glue

Materials

- None

Bonus Idea: If you are unable to visit a garden, bring in an inexpensive plant. Pull up the plant and show them the roots. Show pictures of gardens with and without weeds.

Plant Seeds

Directions: Gather some easy-to-grow seeds, soil, and small pots or plastic cups for the kids. Allow kids to plant seeds. Write the day's Bible story reference on the outside of the pot.

Say: Place this plant somewhere where you will see it every day to remind you that **God wants us to listen to and obey the Bible.**

Pumpkin Seed Art

Preparation: Dye pumpkin seeds with food coloring. Just place seeds and color inside a plastic bag and shake! Spread seeds out on newspaper to dry.

Say: Our Bible story today was all about seeds. Let's make some colorful art work with these seeds to remind us of the day's lesson.

Directions: Using the colorful seeds, encourage kids to make a work of art. To read more, search online for "pumpkin seed art."

Garden Tour

Directions: Walk your church campus to visit a garden and observe the plants. If possible, pull out a plant and observe the roots.

Say: Do you see any weeds? What would happen if the weeds were left to grow? How does this garden relate to the day's Bible story?

Bonus Activity

Preparation: There are many great videos online that provide a quick summary of this parable. Search YouTube for "Jesus parable of the sower" to find one to show the kids.

Say: Let's watch a quick video about the day's lesson to help us remember the different kinds of seeds and soil.

Chapter 40: Workers in the Vineyard

BIBLE STORY REFERENCE: Matthew 20:1–16

MEMORY VERSE: *So the last will be first, and the first will be last. Matthew 20:16*

Big Idea
God Gives Us Mercy

Overview

Say: Jesus told many stories during his time on Earth. He wanted to teach people about God and about the kingdom of God. One day, he told a story about workers in a grape vineyard. Of course, this story wasn't really about a vineyard. It was about the kingdom of God. *(Open with prayer requests, praises, and a time of prayer.)*

Bible Story

Say: Have you ever been paid more than you deserve for a job? How did you feel? *(Children respond.)*

In our Bible story today, the owner of a vineyard was looking for some workers. He hired workers all throughout the day. At the end of the day, everyone received the same wage—whether they worked for an hour or for the entire day. Let's read what happened in Matthew 20:11–15. *(Read Scripture aloud.)*

The vineyard owner was very generous with his money. He paid many of the workers more than they deserved.

In the same way, **God gives us mercy.** When we repent of our sins, God forgives us and welcomes us into his kingdom. You can go to heaven whether you have been saved for many years or whether you get saved just hours before death. Some people might think this is unfair—just like those workers did! But **God gives us mercy** generously. It's not our decision who God gives mercy to, and I sure am glad that he is generous with his mercy.

Outline
Overview
Bible Story
Opening Game
Object Lesson
Additional Optional Activities

Materials
- **Bibles**
- **Bonus Activity: Reproducible page 243**
- **Grapes**
- **Shallow plastic basin**
- **Wall clock that you can easily manipulate**
- **Small toy people**
- **Brown and green felt**
- **Gold coins**
- **6 same-sized containers with lids**
- **Coins**
- **Cardstock**
- **Tacky glue**
- **Purple pony beads**
- **Brown markers**
- **Number cubes**
- **Paper**
- **Pencil**

Opening Game: Grab Those Grapes!

Materials

- Grapes
- Shallow plastic basin

Tip: For extra fun, freeze the grapes ahead of time.

Say: In our Bible story today, the workers were picking grapes with their hands. However, in this game, you're going to need to use your toes!

Directions: Children take off their shoes and socks. Place several handfuls of grapes in a large shallow plastic basin. Kids sit down around the tote. On your mark, kids will reach into the tote with their feet and try to grab grapes with their toes. Have them form a small pile of the grapes they collect. Whoever has the most grapes at the end of one minute recites, or chooses a volunteer to recite, the memory verse.

VOLUNTEER TIDBITS

God has sat with his big drawing canvas and has seen the children who will come into you room this year. He knows the trials of their life and the needs of their heart and soul. He knows what needs to happen to prepare them for what will come. Looking at that array of children, he has perfectly orchestrated a group of volunteers to meet their needs and feed their soul. You will add your unique accent and brush strokes to their lives. You have been prepared and uniquely gifted for this year and these kids. Each of you will contribute a needed resource to the team and the environment.

Turn to page 163 for more Volunteer Tidbits.

Object Lesson: Time to Find Some Workers

Materials

- Wall clock that you can easily manipulate
- Small toy people, about ten
- Brown and green felt
- Gold coins, same number as toy people

Directions: Hold the clock for the kids to see. Read Matthew 20:1–16 to the kids, moving the toy people from the brown felt, representing the marketplace, to the green felt, representing the vineyard. Change the time on the clock according to the story. At the end of the Bible story, when the workers are paid, place one gold coin in front of each figure.

Say: I wonder how the workers felt when they all received the same amount. How would you have felt if you were one of the people who worked all day?

Some people feel the same way about God that these workers did. They think if they do extra work or work all their lives, that they should receive extra rewards from God.

But Jesus explained that God's kingdom doesn't work like that. **God gives us mercy** no matter when we ask for it. He offers the same forgiveness for sins whether we ask for salvation early in our lives or very late in our lives. It might seem unfair, but it's actually very generous of God.

I'm so glad that **God gives us mercy** and that we all can have a chance to go to Heaven because of his mercy.

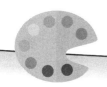

Additional Optional Activities

Materials

- 6 same-sized containers with lids
- Coins

More or Less

Preparation: Place different amounts of coins in each container. Place the lids on the containers.

Say: In our Bible story, the workers got paid the same amount no matter how long they worked. However, in this game, you must sort out containers according to which has more or less.

Directions: Kids shake the containers, listen to the coins inside, and put the containers in order from least to greatest, all within a minute.

Materials

- Cardstock
- Tacky glue
- Purple pony beads
- Brown markers

3-D Grape Vines

Say: Let's make an art project that will remind us of today's parable and God's mercy.

Directions: Children write Matthew 20:1 across the top of a sheet of cardstock. They then draw brown vines, leaving room to glue purple pony beads onto the vines to create grapes.

Materials

- Number cubes, one for each child
- Paper
- Pencil

That's Not Fair!

Say: The workers thought they were being treated unfairly, but God's mercy doesn't always make sense. This game has some crazy rules, too!

Directions: Divide kids up into pairs and give them a sheet of paper to keep score. Give each child a die. Players roll the number cubes at the same time. If the pair gets the same number, no one scores. If they get different numbers, the player with the LOWEST number gets the same number of points as dots on number cube. Pairs keep track of their points. Whenever a player gets to thirty points, they tell, or choose a volunteer to tell, a sentence about the story, and then start over

Turn to page 243 for a Bonus Activity.

Chapter 41: Jesus Died for Our Sins

BIBLE STORY REFERENCE: Mark 15:16–20, Matthew 26:38–39

MEMORY VERSE: *He himself bore our sins in his body on the cross, so that we might die to sins and live for righteousness.* 1 Peter 2:24

Big Idea
Jesus Paid the Price for Our Sins

Overview

Say: Ever since Adam and Eve disobeyed God in the Garden of Eden, sin has been present in the world. Everyone who has ever lived has sinned (Romans 3:23), and that sin separates us from God. God didn't want us to be separate from him, so he sent his Son, Jesus, to rescue us from our sins. During Jesus' time on Earth, he helped many people and taught many things. His true purpose, though, was to pay the price for our sins. He had to do that by dying on the cross. The Bible tells us that the price for sin is death. God sent his Son to pay the price for us. **Jesus paid the price for our sins** by dying on the cross. It was a huge price to pay, but he did it because of his love for us. (*Open with prayer requests, praises, and a time of prayer.*)

Bible Story

Say: Today's Bible story is strange. It's happy because God rescued us from our sins. But it is also very sad because Jesus paid the price for our sins by dying on the cross. Jesus suffered a great deal before and during the time he was crucified. Let's read about it in Mark 15:16–20. (*Children respond.*) It was hard for **Jesus to pay the price for our sins**. Let's read some more in Matthew 26:38–39. (*Read Scripture aloud.*)

Jesus did not want to die, but he did because of his great love for us. Because of Jesus' death and because he rose to life again, we can have a relationship with God, which is definitely something to be happy about.

Outline
Overview
Bible Story
Opening Game
Object Lesson
Additional Optional Activities

Materials
- Bibles
- Cereal boxes
- Pretend bills
- Paid in full stamp
- Video of Jesus' life
- Paper
- Markers or crayons
- Cross
- Medium-sized smooth stone
- Markers
- Buckets
- Water
- Chalk

Opening Game: Building a Bridge

Materials

- Cereal boxes, one for each child

Preparation: Cut the front and back off of each cereal box, creating two pieces for each child.

Say: Our sin separates us from God, but Jesus' death made a way for us to be close to God again. Jesus is like our bridge to God. He made a way to get to God by paying the price for our sins. In this game, we're going to build a bridge using two pieces of cardboard.

Directions: On your signal, kids will step onto one piece and then put the other piece in front of them. They can then step onto the second piece and reposition the first to get closer to the opposite wall. If they step off the cardboard, they start again.

VOLUNTEER TIDBITS

Why are you here? Each one of you was drawn to this ministry for different reasons. Some love children and relate to them easily. Some feel children are our future and it is our calling as a church family to prepare them to stand for God. Some of you felt there was a need and you had the time to fill it. Some are passionate about teaching a love for God's Word and are gifted in that way. OR You may be a big kid at heart and this is the only place you can come and play without a funny look from someone.

Turn to page 167 for more Volunteer Tidbits.

Object Lesson: Paid in Full

Materials
- Pretend bills
- Paid in full stamp

Tip: Use the invoice function on Microsoft Word to print pretend bills.

Say: Do your parents ever get any bills? Do they like paying bills? (*Children respond.*)

People don't usually like paying bills. We have to pay bills for electric and heat. We have to pay bills for a house to live in, and we have to pay for things that we buy like food and things we need around the house. It isn't much fun, but we need to do it in order to have those things.

How do you think people would feel if suddenly, all their bills were paid for? (*Children respond. Loudly stamp the bills with the "paid in full" stamp as the kids give their answers.*) **That would be amazing! I know I would be celebrating! I would feel so free and happy!**

Did you know that Jesus paid an even bigger bill for us? **Jesus paid the price for our sins**! The Bible tells us that the payment for sin is death. (*Read Romans 6:23.*) I don't know about you,

but I definitely don't want to die in order to pay for my sins. But we can't be friends with God unless someone pays this bill for us.

That's why Jesus came to Earth. He paid the price—death—so that we could be friends with God forever. (*Read Romans 4:25.*) **Jesus paid the price for our sins.** The Bible tells us that we can mark our sin bill as "paid in full" if we confess our sins and believe in Jesus Christ as our Savior.

God loves the world—that's you and me! He doesn't want us to keep living with our sin. He sent Jesus to rescue us and to pay the price for our sins. (*Read John 3:16.*) **This is exciting news indeed.**

Directions: Give the children a chance to ask questions and pray with anyone who would like to become a Christian.

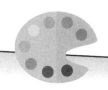

Additional Optional Activities

Materials

- Video of Jesus' life
- Paper
- Markers or crayons

Tip: There are some great videos online that review Jesus' life. Search online for "God's story: Jesus".

Materials

- Cross
- Medium-sized smooth stone, one for each child
- Markers

Materials

- Buckets
- Water
- Chalk

Jesus Is Part of God's Story

Say: Let's take a look at this quick video. After we see the video, take some time to think about what you learned about Jesus. Draw pictures about your favorite things about Jesus.

Directions: Show children video. Give them paper and have them draw pictures of their favorite things about Jesus.

Lay Your Burden at the Cross

Directions: Give children a few quiet moments, and ask them to consider if there is a sin weighing on their heart and mind. On a smooth stone, kids draw a simple picture to represent their sin. Encourage children to pray, asking for forgiveness. Children lay the stone at the cross, knowing that **Jesus paid the price for our sins**.

Say: Keeping sin in our life does not make us feel good. The Bible describes it as a burden too heavy to bear (Psalm 38:4). **Jesus paid the price for our sins** so that we don't have to keep on carrying our burden.

Washing Away Sins

Preparation: Fill a few buckets with water. Leave buckets outside.

Directions: Go outside with the kids. Give each kid a piece of sidewalk chalk. Encourage them to think about their week and draw pictures to represent sins they have committed.

Say: Jesus' death washes away all our sins. Let's dump water on our "sins" until they are gone. Let's celebrate the fact that God forgives and forgets our sins, erasing them completely from our lives.

Chapter 42: The Resurrection

BIBLE STORY REFERENCE: Luke 24:1–8

MEMORY VERSE: *He is not here; he has risen! Luke 24:6*

Overview

Say: Last week we heard a difficult Bible story. It was difficult thinking about how sad Jesus must have been to have to suffer and die. It was hard thinking about how cruel the soldiers were and how much it must have hurt to die on a cross. It's amazing that Jesus was willing to do that. Jesus loves every single person so much that he was willing to pay the price for our sins. Thankfully though, that's not the end of the story! Today, we'll see that **Jesus is more powerful than death**. After Jesus paid the price for our sins, he defeated both sin and death. We can live free from sin and as friends with God because Jesus died and rose again. *(Open with prayer requests, praises, and a time of prayer.)*

Bible Story

Say: Have you ever been so startled or surprised by something that you almost fell over?

In today's Bible story, two women went to visit the tomb where Jesus was buried. They were planning on putting spices on his body, but they got a big surprise when they got there. Let's turn in our Bibles to Luke 24:1–8. *(Read Scripture aloud.)* The women were certainly surprised, and they were thrilled to hear the good news about Jesus.

Outline

Overview
Bible Story
Opening Game
Object Lesson
Additional Optional Activities

Materials

- Bibles
- Blown egg
- Male doll
- Strips of cloth or paper towels
- Essential oils
- Crescent rolls
- Marshmallow
- Butter
- Cinnamon
- Sugar
- Oven or toaster oven
- Plastic knives
- Napkins
- Raw eggs
- Large needle
- Bowl
- Antibacterial soap
- Paper towels
- Permanent markers

Opening Game: Are You Jesus?

Say: Isn't it amazing that Jesus rose from the dead? No one has ever raised themselves from the dead—not before Jesus and not after him. **Jesus is more powerful than death.** After Jesus was resurrected, he saw many people. The strange thing is, many of those people didn't recognize him at first; even though they had been very good friends with Jesus.

In this game, three kids are going to hide. One is going to pretend to be Jesus. Just like the friends didn't recognize Jesus at first, you're not going to know who is pretending to be Jesus and who is just a regular person. You'll have to ask them.

Directions: Choose three volunteers to hide in the room. Whisper to each child whether or not they will pretend to be Jesus. The other kids close their eyes while the hiders hide. When volunteers are hidden, the other children open their eyes and search for the hiders. When a hider is found, kids ask, "Are you Jesus?" If the person says no, they leave the hider where they are and keep looking until the pretend Jesus is found.

VOLUNTEER TIDBITS
Know the Three Types of Lesson Objectives

1. **Cognitive**—A change in what a person knows and understands.
2. **Affective**—A change in attitudes, the way a person feels or responds emotionally. Since you can't see emotions, affective objectives describe actions that can affect emotions.
3. **Psychomotor**—A change in behavior or what a person does with what they know and feel.

Turn to page 171 for more Volunteer Tidbits.

Object Lesson: Empty Egg, Empty Tomb

Materials
• Blown egg

Tip: If you don't know how to blow out an egg, search for a video online.

Say: Who can tell me something about this egg? (*Children respond.*) We use eggs for all kinds of things. They make a tasty breakfast. We use them a lot in baking. Sometimes we just use the egg yolk or the egg white.

This egg is different than the eggs we usually use. Anyone want to guess how it is different? (*Children respond.*) Good guesses. Let's take a look inside. (*Crack the egg open and show the kids the empty inside.*)

Wow! That's pretty surprising! I bet you were not expecting to find an empty egg. That's the same as it was for the people in our Bible story today! Let's take a look. (*Read Luke 24:1–12.*)

Jesus' friends were so surprised to find an empty tomb. After they had seen Jesus, alive and well, they realized that **Jesus is more powerful than death**. Jesus took away our sins when he died on the cross, and I'm so glad that he did not stay dead. When we ask God to forgive our sins and choose to follow Jesus, we can live forever with him in heaven.

Directions: Give the children a chance to ask questions and pray with anyone who would like to become a Christian.

Materials

- Male doll
- Strips of cloth or paper towels
- Essential oils

Materials

- Crescent roll dough
- Marshmallow
- Butter
- Cinnamon
- Sugar
- Oven or toaster oven
- Plastic knives
- Napkins

Materials

- Raw eggs
- Large needle
- Bowl
- Antibacterial soap
- Paper towels
- Permanent markers

Allergy Alert: Post a note to warn parents about the use of eggs in this activity.

Tip: Search online for "permanent marker Easter eggs." Print out pictures to inspire kids drawings.

Wrapped in Linen, Covered in Spices

Say: When people died in Bible times, their bodies were wrapped in cloths and laid in a stone tomb. Often, the bodies were covered in spices and perfumes before the tomb was sealed. Let's do the same!

Directions: In this activity, kids will wrap a male doll (poseable doll would work great) with either strips of cloth or strips of paper towels. Provide a variety of essential oils for the kids to use to then cover the cloth in, pretending to prepare the body for burial.

Resurrection Rolls

Directions: As you prepare this snack, tell children the marshmallow represents the body of Jesus. Kids to put "oil" (butter) and spices (cinnamon and sugar) on the "body" and then wrap it completely in the  crescent roll dough. Place in 350°F oven for ten minutes. Allow rolls to cool. When rolls are cut open, the "body" will be gone—just like Jesus! Give each child a napkin and a roll to enjoy

Blow Eggs and Color

Say: Eggs often remind us of Easter because they symbolize new life. Let's make some decorated eggs today to remind us that **Jesus is more powerful than death.**

Directions: Show kids how to poke a hole in the top and bottom of an egg with a large needle. Blow out the contents into a bowl. After the eggs are blown, washed with antibacterial soap, and dried with paper towels, kids carefully color eggs with permanent markers.

Bonus Activity

The paper plate tomb craft from Chapter 36: Lazarus would also work for this chapter.

Chapter 43: Jesus Gives Final Instructions

BIBLE STORY REFERENCE: Matthew 28:16–20

MEMORY VERSE: *Therefore go and make disciples of all nations, baptizing them in the name of the Father and of the Son and of the Holy Spirit, and teaching them to obey everything I have commanded you. Matthew 28:19–20*

Big Idea
Go and Make Disciples

Overview

Say: When we become a Christian, we chose to follow Christ. We don't always do things right, but our lives are different because the most important thing to us is God. To be a disciple of Christ means to obey his commands and follow his ways. Jesus not only wanted his friends to tell others about him, Jesus wanted them to help people become disciples as well. (*If time permits, share your own brief testimony about when you became a Christian and the ways that you are currently trying to follow Christ. Then open with prayer requests, praises, and a time of prayer.*)

Bible Story

After Jesus died and rose again, he spent a little more time with his disciples. Jesus knew that he would soon be returning to heaven, so he wanted to give some final instructions to the people who had chosen to follow him. Let's read Matthew 28:16–20. (*Read Scripture aloud.*) Jesus told his friend to **go and make disciples**. This is something that we should be doing as well. Jesus promised that he would be with us, even until the end of time. We can boldly share the good news about Jesus' death and resurrection with the people in our lives, knowing that Jesus will help us every step of the way.

Outline
Overview
Bible Story
Opening Game
Object Lesson
Additional Optional Activities

Materials
- **Bibles**
- **Dominoes**
- **Notecards**
- **Markers**
- **Inexpensive journals or composition books**
- **Pencils or pens**
- **Decorating supplies**

Opening Game: Follow the Leader

Say: "Disciple" is another word for follower. In this game, we'll follow the leader, walking or moving in whatever way they do.

Directions: Pick a leader to begin the game and have the rest of the kids line up behind them. Allow them to be the leader, acting and moving however they like around the room and instructing the others to follow along. After about 30 seconds, pick a new leader. Continue this pattern until game time is up.

Say: We followed the leader with our physical movements in this game, but Jesus wants his disciples to follow him with their whole lives. This means the way we act, talk, and even think should be according to Jesus' instructions. It's not always easy, but through God's strengths, we can continue to grow as we become disciples of Christ.

VOLUNTEER TIDBITS

Write down how you feel you are uniquely gifted to contribute to the children you will encounter in the year to come. Pray that you will yield to the Lord each week to be used by him to impact children for the kingdom.

Turn to page 175 for more Volunteer Tidbits.

Object Lesson: Dominos Disciples

Materials

- Dominoes

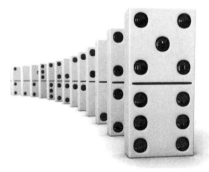

Say: Today, we're going to imagine that these dominoes are actually people. (*Hold up one domino and ask the kids to help you pick out a name for the domino.*)

This person is named (Marcus). One day (Marcus) was talking to his grandpa who told him all about Jesus. (Marcus) loved hearing this good news and quickly decided to follow Jesus. He became a disciple. (*Set the domino up carefully on the table so it is standing upright.*)

In fact, (Marcus) was so excited about Jesus that he told his next door neighbor, named . . . (*Hold up another domino and ask kids to name it.*) (Sami)! (Sami) had heard about Jesus before, but he had never made a decision to follow him. Well, that day (Sami) did make a decision to follow Jesus. (*Set up domino carefully on the table so it is standing upright next to the other domino.*)

(Sami) went to church and heard that we are to **go and make disciples**, so he began thinking about who he could tell about Jesus. (Sami) had a friend at karate class that he decided to invite to church. That friend was named . . . (*Hold up another domino and ask kids to name it.*) (Rhianna)! (Rhianna) came to church with (Sami) for a few months and one day, she decided to pray and become forever friends with God. (*Set up domino carefully on the table so it is standing upright next to the other dominos.*)

(Rhianna) was so excited about her friendship with God. It really changed her life! In fact, her parents saw such a big difference that they decided to become friends with God, too. (*Set up two more dominos carefully on the table so they are standing upright next to the other dominos.*)

This continued to happen until many more people (*Continue setting up more dominoes.*) **heard about Jesus.** It all started with one person who told another, who told another, and so on. (*Tap the dominoes to make them all fall in a chain reaction.*) You could cause the same effect. Jesus tells us to **go and make disciples**, and that starts by telling the people around us!

Additional Optional Activities

Message from a Missionary

Say: Missionaries are people who have dedicated their lives to making disciples of all nations. They often move to a new country, learn a new language, learn a new way of living, and work in many ways to tell the people around them about Jesus. Let's hear from one now.

Preparation: If you have a connection to a missionary, see if you can get an update of their work or talk to them over a video-conferencing application during class. If not, search online for "short missionary stories for children" to share with the group.

Prayer for a Friend

Directions: Encourage kids to think of people in their lives who do not yet follow Jesus. Write these friends' names down on notecards.

Say: God brought these friends into your life for a reason. Since we are all instructed to **go and make disciples**, it might be God's plan for you to share the good news with your friend. Let's commit to praying for these people daily and ask God to give you an opportunity to share the good news. Let's pray now!

Daily Disciplines

Say: Jesus regularly took time to pray and to read the Bible. As a disciple of Jesus, we should follow this practice. Let's think of ways that we can develop a daily habit of Bible reading and prayer.

Directions: Talk with kids about having a quiet time with God and journaling. Have kids take a few minutes alone to write a few thoughts in their journal about the day's lesson. Provide decorating supplies for kids to use on the front of their books.

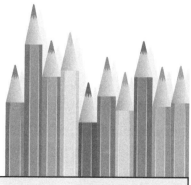

Materials

- Notecards
- Markers

Materials

- Inexpensive journals or composition books, one for each child
- Pencils or pens
- Decorating supplies (stickers, markers, etc.)

Optional: Show children some age-appropriate Bibles that might be good to use in their quiet times.

Turn to page 244 for a Bonus Activity.

Chapter 44: The Holy Spirit Comes

BIBLE STORY REFERENCE: Acts 1:4–5, 2:1–12

MEMORY VERSE: *You will receive power when the Holy Spirit comes on you. Acts 1:8*

Overview

Say: After the Resurrection, Jesus spent a little more time on Earth before he returned to heaven. One day, when he was eating with them, Jesus told them that he would be sending a gift to them. It would be the gift of the Holy Spirit. (*Read Acts 1:4–5.*) Forty days after Jesus' resurrection, Jesus returned to heaven. The disciples were probably wondering what they should do next. They continued to meet together as a group. One day, something amazing happened. The disciples received the gift that Jesus had promised! The disciples were **filled with the Holy Spirit and were about do amazing things through his power.** (*Open with prayer requests, praises, and a time of prayer.*)

Bible Story

Say: Does anyone know how to speak another language? (*Children respond.*)

When the disciples were filled with the Holy Spirit, they were able to do some pretty amazing things. They had the power through the Holy Spirit to speak in different languages! Let's read about that amazing day in Acts 2:1–12. (*Read Scripture aloud.*) After this, the disciples began boldly preaching about Jesus and many people became disciples of Christ.

Outline
Overview
Bible Story
Opening Game
Object Lesson
Additional Optional Activities

Materials
• Bibles
• Reproducible page 245
• Inflated balloons
• Fans
• Trick candle
• Lighter
• Construction paper
• Tape
• Markers
• Ice
• Water
• Black construction paper
• Red, orange, yellow tissue paper
• Glue

Opening Game: Mighty Rushing Wind

Materials

- Inflated balloons, one for each child
- Fans

Bonus Idea: Create teams and see which team can keep it going longest.

Directions: Give each child an inflated balloon. Set up a few rotating fans in the room, turn on the ceiling fan, or open windows to create a strong air flow. Instruct kids to try and keep the balloons in the air for as long as possible by hitting them upward (no holding balloons!). Last child to have their balloon hit the ground tells, or chooses a volunteer to tell, a sentence about the Bible story.

Say: The Bible tells us that when the Holy Spirit came, there was a sound like a mighty rushing wind that filled the room. In this game, we're going to create some of our own wind while we try to keep balloons in the air.

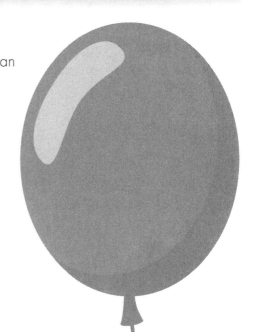

VOLUNTEER TIDBITS

Imagine if all the Godly truths you share truly sank in. Imagine the assurance and confidence they would have to overcome the lies, doubts, and fears. What you do guides them to the One who knows them, loves them, and can transform them. Showing them, in Christ, they belong, are beautiful, strong, and loved!

Turn to page 179 for more Volunteer Tidbits.

Object Lesson: Can't Put Out the Flame

Materials

- Trick candle, like those used on birthday cakes
- Lighter

Say: Who can tell me about this? (*Children respond.*) We usually use this for a special occasion like a birthday. However, today, it's going to help us learn a little bit more about the Holy Spirit. The Bible tells us that the disciples were gathered together one day when suddenly the sound of a mighty wind filled the room and something appeared over their heads that looked like flames of a fire. (*Read Acts 2:1–3.*)

(*Light the candle.*) It was amazing! The gift that Jesus had promised had come to the disciples. Jesus told them they would receive power from the Holy Spirit to tell people all about Jesus. (*Read Acts 1:8.*)

Immediately, the disciples began telling others about Jesus—and everyone heard in their own language! That's pretty amazing. But some people tried to put an end to things. They said the disciples had too much wine to drink. They tried to make it seem like the disciples were acting crazy. (*Blow out the candle.*)

But we know that's not true. (*Candle should relight itself.*) **The Holy Spirit gives us power**. He gave the disciples power to speak boldly.

After the people made fun of them, Peter got up and began to tell the whole story about Jesus. After he finished talking to the people, the people were really impacted. (*Read Acts 2:37.*) Peter told them what to do. (*Read Acts 2:38–39.*) After this time, many people tried to stop the disciples from sharing the good news of Jesus (*Blow out candle.*), but because of the Holy Spirit (*Candle should relight.*), they were unstoppable! The Holy Spirit gives us power, too. We can share the good news of Jesus wherever we go.

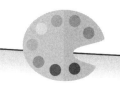

Additional Optional Activities

Materials

- Construction paper, various colors
- Tape
- Markers

Create a Hand Fan

Say: Let's create a hand fan to remind you of the wind of the Holy Spirit.

Directions: Using construction paper, fold the paper about every inch, accordion style. Kids may want to draw a design on their fan before or after folding. Once the design is complete, tape the bottom of the paper together to create a handle.

Materials

- Ice
- Water

Three Persons of God

Say: God is mysterious. There are three persons, but all one God. The three persons of God are sort of like water. God the father is like ice, Jesus is like liquid water, and the Holy Spirit is like steam. They are all water, but they function differently and are used for different purposes.

Directions: Kids play with ice and water.

Materials

- Reproducible page 245
- Black construction paper
- Red, orange, yellow tissue paper
- Glue

Flames Headbands

Preparation: Copy page 245, making one for each child.

Say: Let's create headbands to illustrate what it may have looked like in the upper room that day.

Directions: Using the reproducible page as a template, children cut out a headband from black construction paper and cut flame shapes from the colors of tissue paper. Glue the flame to the front of the headband.

Chapter 45: The Early Church

BIBLE STORY REFERENCE: Acts 2:42–47

Memory Verse: *They devoted themselves to the apostles' teaching and to fellowship, to the breaking of bread and to prayer. Acts 2:42*

**Big Idea
Our Things Are
for Sharing**

Overview

Say: After the disciples received the Holy Spirit, they boldly shared the good news of Jesus with others. Many people came to believe in Jesus. They became disciples of Jesus, too. These disciples met together regularly and helped each other however they could. They realized that **our things are for sharing**. They were more concerned about helping each other than hanging onto their things. In the same way, when God blesses us with things in our lives, he wants us to share and be generous with others. (*Open with prayer requests, praises, and a time of prayer.*)

Bible Story

Say: What is the hardest part about sharing with others? (*Children respond.*)

The early church wanted to make sure everyone was taken care of, so they did some pretty unusual things. (*Read Acts 2:42–47.*) These early Christians believed that **our things are for sharing.** God blessed them when they acted this way. More and more people became Christians every day. That's pretty exciting!

Outline
Overview
Bible Story
Opening Game
Object Lesson
Additional Optional Activities

Materials
- Bibles
- Soft ball or stuffed animal
- Goldfish crackers
- Rolls or bread slices

Opening Game: Sharing Potato

Materials
- Soft ball or stuffed animal

Say: In the early church, sharing was a big deal. The Bible tells us that these disciples of Christ shared everything they had. In this game, we're going to practice sharing by passing along this object.

Directions: Have kids sit in a circle facing each other. Begin by giving one person a soft ball or stuffed animal. Play some music and instruct children to begin passing the object to their right. Traditionally, when the music stops, whoever is holding the "potato" loses and has to sit out for the rest of the round. However, in this game, we're going to give a point to the person who has just passed on (or shared) the "potato" when the music stops. Play the music for 10–20 seconds for the kids. When the music stops, say to the person to the left of the "potato," "Way to go! You just shared that object. You get a point!" Continue playing as time allows.

VOLUNTEER TIDBITS

Children are fed a steady stream of information from the world. YOU are part of the Godly initiative to counter those voices that lie. Your commitment tells these children, "You are valuable!" "We care for you!" "You are an important part of our family!" "We are invested in you!"

Turn to page 183 for more Volunteer Tidbits.

Object Lesson: Crackers To Share

Materials

- Goldfish crackers

Say: I'm going to be passing some things out, but I want you to leave them alone until the end of the lesson.

In the early church, the disciples of Christ met regularly. The Bible tells us that they helped each other and they often ate meals together. (*Read Acts 2:42–47.*)

Some of the people in the group had a lot of things (*Give one child ten to twelve goldfish.*), and some people didn't have much at all. (*Give another child one or two goldfish.*) Some people probably didn't even have anything at all. (*Shrug your shoulders at the remaining children.*)

These early disciples of Christ could have said something like, "Well, I worked hard and I earned my stuff. I'm keeping what I've got." But they didn't do that. They realized that **our things are for sharing.**

They began to notice that some people among them probably had way more than they needed (*Give a child about twenty goldfish.*), and some probably had just the right amount. (*Give several children four or five goldfish.*)

They decided that together, as a team, they were going to make sure that everyone had just what they needed. That's what you're going to do right now, too. Remembering that our things are for sharing, let's work together to make sure everyone in the room has something to eat.

Directions: Kids sort out the goldfish, distributing as they see fit. Try to not interfere unless really necessary. After they have divided it among themselves, go around and add to the piles if they seem small.

Say: Good job sharing with the group. What was the hardest part about this? (*Children respond.*) Sometimes it's hard to share, especially if it seems like there isn't going to be much to go around. **Our things are for sharing.** God gave us everything we currently have and he is pleased when we share our things with others.

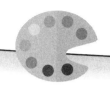

Additional Optional Activities

Materials

- None

Bonus Idea: Instead of an exchange, arrange to have the children bring in toys for a local homeless shelter. Children include notes of encouragement to the children receiving the toys.

Materials

- None

Tip: Operation Christmas Child is a great organization to consider donating to. Money raised from the sale can be used to buy supplies to fill the shoeboxes.

Toy Exchange

Say: Just like the early Christians shared their things, let's practice sharing by switching toys with others.

Directions: Many of the kids in your group may have toys that they no longer like or play with. Consider organizing a toy exchange where kids can practice sharing their things with others. Have each child bring a toy they no longer want to the event. In exchange, they get to leave with a new toy from another child. You may want to bring a few toys from your own home to increase the selection.

Selling Our Things

Say: The early Christians sold their things and used the money to help others. Let's do the same by organizing a yard sale!

Directions: Consider hosting a yard sale at your church to benefit a local charity or organization. Church members and families bring in their things to sell, and all the profits from the sale will be donated to those in need.

Materials

- Rolls or bread slices

Tip: In consideration of gluten-free children, also provide large gluten-free crackers or bread.

Breaking Bread and Prayer

Directions: Provide some rolls or slices of bread for the kids to snack on and spend some time praying for one another.

Say: One of the things the disciples did regularly was break bread, or eat, together and pray. Let's do the same, remembering to pray for friends who do not follow Christ yet, for people who may be sick, for leaders, friends, and family.

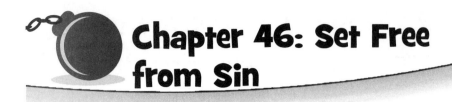

Chapter 46: Set Free from Sin

BIBLE STORY REFERENCE: Romans 6:16–18

MEMORY VERSE: *You have been set free from sin. Romans 6:18*

**Big Idea
God Set Us
Free from Sin**

Overview

Say: The book of Romans was written by a man named Paul. It was a letter written to the Christians living in Rome during that time. Paul wanted to encourage the Christians to keep following God and doing the right thing. He told them many things in the book of Romans, but one thing was the fact that **God set us free from sin**. He explained that before Jesus saves us from our sins (salvation), it is like we are slaves to sin. We can't get free. But because Jesus defeated sin and death on the cross, we don't have to keep living like that! When we believe in Jesus and accept his free gift of salvation, we stop being slaves to sin. This freedom is amazing and certainly something to celebrate! (*Open with prayer requests, praises, and a time of prayer.*)

Bible Story

Say: Have you ever been stuck somewhere? How did it feel? How did it feel after you were free? (*Children respond.*)

It doesn't feel good to be stuck! Whether you're stuck in the snow in a car or stuck behind a couch, it's no fun. In our Bible story, Paul explains that we are stuck in our sin before we know Jesus as our Savior. Let's read about it in Romans 6:16–18. (*Read Scripture aloud.*)

I don't like the idea of sin being my master! The good news is that it doesn't have to stay that way! **God set us free from sin** through Jesus' death on the cross. We don't have to live as slaves anymore. We can be free from sin through Jesus' actions and God's power.

Outline

**Overview
Bible Story
Opening Game
Object Lesson
Additional Optional Activities**

Materials

- **Bibles**
- **Large square cardboard box**
- **Large black marker**
- **White construction paper**
- **Strips of cloth**
- **Scissors**
- **Chair**
- **Toilet paper**
- **Many strips of paper**
- **Markers**

Opening Game: Which Way?

Materials

- Large square cardboard box
- Large black marker
- White construction paper

Preparation: Create a large die ahead of time by drawing black circles on a large square box. Write "Sin" on a sheet of construction paper and "Righteousness" on a second sheet. Place a signs on opposite walls of the playing area.

Say: In our Bible story today, Paul talks about being a slave to sin or slave to righteousness, or doing right things. When you are a slave, you have to obey whatever your master says. Sin only leads to death, but righteousness leads to eternal life. If we try to defeat sin on our own, we can't do it. We might be able to succeed for awhile, but soon we have to obey our sinful master again. **Only God can set us free from sin**. In this game, we will demonstrate what it's like to try to defeat sin with our own power.

Directions: Have kids line up in the middle of the room. Begin the game by rolling the die. If the number is EVEN, kids walk that number of steps towards the righteousness sign.

If the number is ODD, kids walk that number of steps towards the sin sign. End the game before they reach either wall.

Say: Was it frustrating to never reach a destination? That's how life is like when we try to live in our own power. We can't be free from sin by ourselves. Thankfully, **God set us free from sin.** We don't have to live like this! We can live in true freedom and live a life of righteousness with God's strength and power.

VOLUNTEER TIDBITS

Spiritual change happens over time when our faith community is willing to pour the Word into the lives of our children.

Turn to page 187 for more Volunteer Tidbits.

Object Lesson: Free from Sin

Materials

- Strips of cloth
- Scissors
- Chair

Preparation: Cut cloth strips from old sheet. Ask an adult volunteer to sit in a chair.

Say: What is the first story in the Bible? (*Children respond.* It was the true story of Adam and Eve.

In the beginning of time, things were great. Everything was just as it should be. But things didn't stay perfect for long. Eve chose to listen to a sneaky snake instead of God's rules. And Adam followed right after Eve!

Because both Adam and Eve disobeyed God's one and only rule, they had to leave the perfect garden. Ever since then, people have been messing things up pretty bad. People hurt one other, they steal, they lie, and they say really mean things. In fact, people, in general, are kind of a mess. I do things wrong, and I bet sometimes you make some bad choices, too. What are some of the bad choices we might make? (*Children respond. As they do, gently wrap the cloth strips around the volunteer's arms, tying them to the chair. Do not tie knots in the cloths.*)

Oh, no. Look what sin is doing to our friend here. We didn't realize it, but the sin is trapping them. They're stuck. And that's exactly how sin works. (*Read Romans 6:16–18.*)

Satan doesn't want us to be free. He wants us to be slaves to sin. He wants us to be stuck in our sin. Thankfully, we don't have to stay like that! **God set us free from sin** through Jesus' death on the cross. Jesus paid the price for our sins and because of that, we don't have to be slaves anymore. (*Read Romans 6:20–23.*)

Directions: Cut the strips of cloth (carefully!) with the scissors. As you snip each piece, say "**God set us free from sin**" out loud. Celebrate that the volunteer is now set free and end with prayer, thanking God for the gift of freedom through salvation.

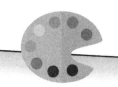

Additional Optional Activities

Materials
- Toilet paper

Materials
- Many strips of paper
- Markers

Note: The "Create in me a Clean Heart" activity from Chapter 17: David as King would also work well for this chapter.

Memory Verse Motions

Say: The Bible tells us that sin leads to death, but following after God leads to life. Let's work together to create motions for this verse to remember that **God set us free from sin**.

Directions: Work with the kids to create motions for Romans 6:23. Take pictures of kids doing the motions and assemble into a poster for them to see next week.

Break Free from Sin

Say: Sin is a tricky thing. It can start out not seeming too bad, but if we allow it to continue in our life, we quickly become trapped. Let's experiment with wrapping each other's hands to see how much toilet paper it takes to become trapped.

Directions: Kids wrap each other's hands in toilet paper to represent being bound by sin.

Say: With only a little toilet paper, it seems easy to break free from sin. However, the longer we let sin live in our lives, the harder it becomes.

Paper Chains

Preparation: Prepare strips of paper for the kids to create paper chains. In Bibles, mark some of the memory verses from this book for the kids to copy in case they have trouble thinking of their own.

Say: God set us free from sin because he wants us to do the right thing. The Bible gives us instructions on how to do the right thing. Let's write our favorite verses on the strips of paper and then turn them into a paper chain.

Turn to page 246 for a Bonus Activity.

Chapter 47: The Body of Christ

BIBLE STORY REFERENCE: 1 Corinthians 12:12–14

MEMORY VERSE: *Now you are the body of Christ, and each one of you is a part of it.* 1 Corinthians 12:27

**Big Idea
God Wants Us to
Work Together**

Overview

Say: Another set of letters written by Paul was written to the church in Corinth (near modern-day Greece). This is where we get the books of 1 and 2 Corinthians. Paul wrote many things in these letters. One thing he wrote was that the church is a like a body. Just like a body works together to function, **God wants us to work together, too.**

(Open with prayer requests, praises, and a time of prayer.)

Bible Story

Say: Do any of you play on a team? Is it easy to work together? *(Children respond.)*

It's not always easy to work together, but things definitely go better as team when we do! In the same way, **God wants us to work together.** Paul explained that everything in a person's body works together to function properly—just like a team. If one part of the body refused to help, everything would go wrong!

Let's read about it in 1 Corinthians 12:12–14. *(Read Scripture aloud.)* **God wants us to work together,** and everyone has an important part to play.

Outline
Overview
Bible Story
Opening Game
Object Lesson
Additional Optional Activities

Materials
- Bibles
- Packs of gum
- Poster board
- Brown and yellow paint
- Paintbrush
- Markers
- Scissors
- Mini prebaked pizza crusts
- Pizza toppings
- Baking sheets
- Bible dictionary or atlas
- Bible-times map
- Decorated puzzle pieces from Object Lesson

Opening Game: Those Aren't My Arms!

Materials

- Packs of gum, one for each pair of players

Bonus Idea: For extra fun, blindfold the second child. If time permits, have kids switch places and play again.

Say: Usually, our bodies work pretty well. When we want to pick something up, our brain sends a signal to our arm or hand and we reach out to pick it up. However, in this game, we're going to see what it would be like if our hand didn't always do what we wanted it to!

Directions: For this game, kids form pairs to unwrap packs of gum in a very unconventional way. Before playing, have all the children wash their hands.

One child from each pair stands in front of a table with hands on hips. The second child (partner) stands behind the first one and puts their arms through the arms of the first child. Only the second child will be allowed to use their hands in the activity.

Place a packet of gum on the table, one pack in front of each pair. The second child in each pair picks up the gum, unwraps a piece, and puts the gum in the first child's mouth. The first child can give instructions, but cannot move their own arms or hands.

VOLUNTEER TIDBITS

When you think of opportunities that come along to serve, you typically want your effort to positively impact the soul or life of people in the world.

- What difference can one person make?
- Can you think of key people or moments in time that impacted you?
- Did you see God's hand in those situations?

Turn to page 191 for more Volunteer Tidbits.

Object Lesson: Pizza Dreams

Materials
- Poster board
- Brown and yellow paint
- Paintbrush
- Markers
- Scissors

Preparation: Before class, prepare a poster-board pizza by painting a brown ring on a poster board (crust) with a yellow circle inside (cheese). If you have more than eight kids in your group, prepare two poster board pizzas.

Say: How many kids around here like pizza? (*Children respond.*) Pizza is a favorite food for many people. One of the great things about is that you can personalize it with toppings. You can add nearly whatever you want to it! I've got a pizza here that needs some personalizing!

Directions: Bring the poster-board pizza out and cut it into the same number of slices as you have kids. Pass the slices to the kids along with some crayons or markers. Children draw whatever toppings they want on their pizza. After they are done, assemble the pieces back into the whole pizza.

Say: All of these pieces look so different, but they are still part of this one pizza.

That's how it is with the church. We are all very different. We have different things we can do well (talents), we have different interests, different types of families, and may even live in different school zones.

However, even though we're very different, we're all part of one big church. **God wants us to work together,** using all our different talents and interests to make the church the best it can be. Just like our slices worked together to complete the pizza, **God wants us to work together** to help the church function and to help others with what we do at church.

Additional Optional Activities

Materials

- Mini prebaked pizza crusts
- Pizza toppings: sauce, shredded cheese, pepperoni, onions, pineapples, peppers
- Baking sheets

Pizza Time!

Fresh & Delicious
PIZZA TIME!

ENJOY
~Have a bite~

Say: Let's make a tasty treat today that reminds us of the object lesson and that **God wants us to work together.**

Directions: Kids make their own personal pan pizzas. Mini prebaked crusts can be purchased at groceries stores. Set up a variety of toppings such as sauce, shredded cheese, pepperoni, onions, pineapples, and peppers for the kids to choose from. After they have created their pizzas, bake them about ten minutes in a 350°F oven.

Materials

- Bible dictionary or atlas
- Bible-times map

Bonus Idea: Find maps of all of Paul's journeys to show the children.

Where in the World Is Paul?

Say: Paul took many journeys to tell people about Jesus. He traveled to Antioch, Lystra, Greece, Rome and many other places. Let's take a closer look at some of his adventures.

Directions: Get a Bible dictionary or atlas to read about Paul's journeys and possibly mark them on a modern day map. If you don't have access to these cool Bible tools, search online for "Paul's journeys" for some good resources.

Materials

- Decorated puzzle pieces from Object Lesson, page 188

Reassemble that Pizza

Say: Who thinks they can put this pizza back together? Let's give it a try as I keep time for each player!

Directions: After the object lesson, play a game with the decorated pizza slices. Have the kids race against the clock to see who can reassemble the pizza slices the fastest.

Chapter 48: Armor of God

BIBLE STORY REFERENCE: Ephesians 6:10–18

MEMORY VERSE: *Put on the full armor of God, so that you can take your stand against the devil's schemes. Ephesians 6:11*

Big Idea
We Can Win Against Sin

Overview

Say: A Christian named Paul wrote many letters during his lifetime. Some of these letters became books of our Bible, such as Corinthians, Galatians, and Ephesians. This week, we'll be taking a closer look at the book of Ephesians, which was written to the church at Ephesus. In this book, Paul wrote about many things including how becoming a Christian changes us and how **we can win against sin**. Paul wrote about the armor of God, which allows us to stand strong in Christ. (*Open with prayer requests, praises, and a time of prayer.*)

Bible Story

Say: Do you ever struggle to do the right thing? What kinds of things are hard for you to do? (*Children respond.*)

It's not always easy to do the right thing. The Bible tells us that the devil tries to trick us into doing the wrong thing (*Read Ephesians 6:11–12.*), but through God's power, **we can win against sin.** God gives us a set of armor that will help us fight against sin. Now, this isn't regular armor. It is spiritual armor. It protects us against spiritual attacks from Satan. Let's read about it in Ephesians 6:10–18. (*Read Scripture aloud.*) Each piece of armor protects us or helps us fight in a special way. We'll talk more about the armor later, but let's remember that by God's power, **we can win against sin.**

Outline
Overview
Bible Story
Opening Game
Object Lesson
Additional Optional Activities

Materials
• Bibles
• Reproducible page 248
• Armor of God props
• Protective sports equipment
• Paper
• Markers
• Empty paper towel rolls
• Ping-Pong balls
• Colored paper tape

Opening Game: The Armor of God

Materials

- Armor of God props (costume helmet or winter hat for the helmet of salvation, toy sword for the Bible, etc.)

THE ARMOR OF GOD

Say: By putting on the armor of God, **we can win against sin**. Let's get these soldiers ready for battle by putting on some armor.

Directions: In this game, one child will serve as the model for each team. The rest of the kids will run in the race. Have the model child stand on one end of the playing area and have the props you gathered next to them. Before the race begins, showcase each piece, briefly explaining what is called, reminding kids that **we can win against sin** with the armor of God. Have two teams race to put all the armor of God on the volunteer model.

VOLUNTEER TIDBITS

It is good to know that God has planned you for this moment in time. Each step of your spiritual journey has been designed by God. He brought people into your path to impact you just like you will impact these children.

Turn to page 195 for more Volunteer Tidbits.

Object Lesson: Get Your Gear On

Materials

• Protective sports equipment

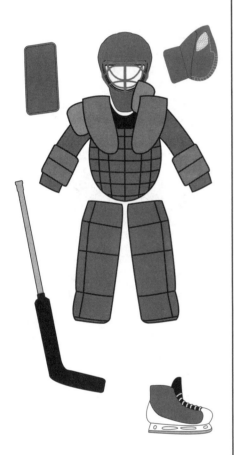

Say: Does anyone here play a sport? Do you have to wear equipment to keep you safe? (*Children respond.*) **In most sports, there is some kind of gear to help protect the player.** (*Hold up the equipment that you brought, describing how it protects the player.*)

Just like we need protection in sports, we need something to keep us safe spiritually. God has provided us with armor to help us fight against our true enemy, Satan. (*Read Ephesians 6:14–17.*) **That's a lot of armor! Let's take a closer look at a few pieces.** (*If you have coordinating sports gear, hold it up when you discuss the companion armor piece.*)

Belt of Truth: The belt of a Roman Soldier held his sword (In this case the Sword of the Spirit). When we live a truthful life with God and others, the Spirit in us is at the ready to do whatever needs to be done.

Breastplate of righteousness: The breastplate protected a soldier's heart. When we chose not to do the right thing (when we chose sin over righteousness), we hurt our hearts. We turn them toward evil instead of God.

Shoes of peace: Just like we can't leave the house without shoes on, a soldier isn't ready to fight without his feet protected. The best way we can prepare for spiritual battle is to be at peace with God, which means confessing and turning away from sin when it sneaks into our lives.

Shield of faith: When we have faith in God, we won't fall for the lies (flaming arrows) of Satan.

Helmet of salvation: Our heads definitely need to be protected in battle! Salvation changes our minds and helps us to see the damage of sin clearly. ·

Sword of the Spirit: With this piece of armor, we can not only protect ourselves, we can fight back! **We can win against sin** by fighting with Bible verses and God's commands.

God has equipped us to fight. **We can win against sin** by preparing ourselves spiritually and trusting in God's power.

Materials

- Paper
- Markers

Bonus Idea: You can also create custom bingo cards by searching online for "free bingo card generator."

Materials

- Reproducible page 248
- Markers

Materials

- Empty paper towel rolls, one for each child
- Ping-Pong balls
- Colored paper tape

Armor of God Bingo

Preparation: Draw a simple Bingo grid or print one from online. Make a copy of the Bingo grid, one for each child.

Say: I'm going to be calling out some words and phrases from our Bible story today. Color in your cards as I call out the words or cover them with buttons as I call out. First player to get five in a row (a bingo!) tells a sentence about the Bible story.

Directions: Kids fill in the grids with words or phrases from the Bible story such as "helmet of salvation," "gospel of peace," "shield of faith," "stand firm," etc. Write the same words and phrases on slips of paper, and drop the slips into a bowl. Distribute the cards to the kids and draw words out of the bowl, one by one.

Coloring Page

Say: Let's color this page to remind us to put on the armor of God. Then let's pray together, asking God to equip us with the armor of God so **we can win against sin**.

Directions: Make a copy of page 248 for each child. Encourage them to color the page and hang it somewhere where they will see it every day.

Battling Sin

Directions: Begin by giving each child an empty paper towel roll "sword." Divide the room in half marking the line with the paper tape. Divide the kids into two even teams. Have each team stand on their side of the battlefield (they cannot cross the center line). Scatter Ping-Pong balls all over the battlefield. Using only their swords to touch the balls (no hands or feet!), kids must try to hit the Ping-Pong balls to the opposing team's side. Set the timer for two to five minutes. At the end of that time, everyone must freeze. The team with the least amount of balls on their side of the battlefield at the end tells a way to win against sin.

Chapter 49: Living as Christians

BIBLE STORY REFERENCE: 1 Thessalonians 5:11–13

MEMORY VERSE: Therefore encourage one another and build each other up, just as in fact you are doing. 1 Thessalonians 5:11

**Big Idea
Love and Encourage
Each Other**

Overview

Say: In the book of 1 Thessalonians, Paul wrote about many things including living to please God and how we should treat each other as Christians. Paul instructed that we should **love and encourage each other**. As Christians, we should try our best to say kind things to each other and build each other up. It's not always easy. Sometimes we want to make fun of others or say something to make them feel bad, but it hurts God when we do this. As Christians, we have the love of God inside of us. We share that love when we **love and encourage each other**. (*Open with prayer requests, praises, and a time of prayer.*)

What to Say

Say: Have you ever been shown a great act of love or encouragement? Tell me about it. (*Children respond. Be prepared with an age-appropriate example of your own.*)

Sometimes a simple word of encouragement can turn your whole day around! Maybe you're struggling with learning a new skill or figuring out a problem. Just having someone say "You can do it!" helps us to keep going. Paul writes about the importance of treating each other well in 1 Thessalonians. Let's read about it in 1 Thessalonians 5:11–13. (*Read Scripture aloud.*) **I love to be encouraged and I love to share God's love and encourage others** as well!

Outline

**Overview
Bible Story
Opening Game
Object Lesson
Additional Optional Activities**

Materials

- Bibles
- Paper
- Pencils
- 3 small cups
- Water
- Food coloring
- Clear plastic cups
- Eye droppers
- Bread slices
- Honey
- Stapler
- Sheets of paper
- Pencils
- Crayons or markers

Opening Activity: What I Like about You

Materials
- Paper
- Pencils

Directions: In this activity, kids will be able to practice **loving and encouraging each other** through kind words. Children sit around a table. Hand each child a sheet of paper. Kids write their names at the top of the paper. Then, everyone passes their paper to the right.

Say: It's time to practice **loving and encouraging others!** Write or draw something encouraging or loving for the child whose name is at the top of the paper in front of you. It could be a happy memory, something that child is talented at, or something positive about their personality. After you have written something, pass the papers again to the right.

Directions: When everyone in the group has had a chance to write something positive and encouraging about everyone else, collect the papers. Read them to make sure everything is indeed positive and then redistribute to the appropriate people.

VOLUNTEER TIDBITS

It is good for us to remember how God sees us. Often times we feel inadequate. We won't do everything right, but even in our weakness God is strong. Ephesians 1:1–14 tells us how he sees us and what we should know about ourselves.

Turn to page 199 for more Volunteer Tidbits.

Object Lesson: Spreading Encouragement

Materials
- 3 small cups
- Water
- Food coloring

THEREFORE
encourage
ONE ANOTHER AND
BUILD EACH OTHER UP,
just as
in fact
you are doing.
1 Thessalonians 5:11

Preparation: Fill two cups halfway with water. Fill remaining cup completely with water.

Say: What is one way that we can encourage someone else? (*Children respond.*) Those are all great ideas. Sometimes we think we have to do big things to really make a difference in someone's life, but often, even the smallest act of **love and encouragement** makes a big impact. (*Read 1 Thessalonians 5:11.*)

Let's imagine today that these three cups of water are three different people. This food coloring is an act of love or encouragement. It could be something simple like holding the door open for someone, giving a team mate a high five during a game, helping your younger sibling with a project, or giving a friend a hug.

Directions: Place two or three drops of food coloring into the full glass of water as you name encouraging acts. Pause a moment to watch the color disperse throughout the water.

Say: Wow! Look what happens when we love and encourage each other. Even one act of encouragement can affect a person in a big way. I love that! And you know what is even cooler? Because this person is feeling so loved and encouraged, they will probably share some encouragement with someone else. (*Pour some of the water into the next glass, again watching as the color disperses.*) What do you think might happen next?

That's right—that person will probably **love and encourage someone else** (*Pour water into third glass.*) and on the cycle goes. God sure knew what he was talking about when he told us to love and encourage each other.

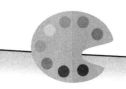

Materials

- Food coloring
- Clear plastic cups
- Eye droppers

Tip: Smocks and gloves may be recommended to keep hands and clothes from changing color.

Materials

- Bread slices
- Honey

Allergy Alert: Children allergic to bees may react to honey. Post a sign letting parents know you are going to serve honey.

Materials

- Stapler
- Sheets of paper
- Pencils
- Crayons or markers

Note: The activities from Chapter 37: The Good Samaritan would also work well for this lesson.

Color Mixing

Say: In this fun activity, we'll be using food coloring and water to remind us of the object lesson and the importance of encouraging others.

Directions: Kids love to see the color mixing effects of food coloring in water. Provide small containers of water (clear plastic cups work great), food coloring, and eye droppers for kids to experiment with. Be sure to provide smocks to protect clothing.

Sweet Like Honey

Say: Proverbs 16:24 tells us that "Kind words are like honey— sweet to the soul and healthy for the body." Let's enjoy a snack that reminds us of the sweetness of kind words.

Directions: Bring in some bread slices or biscuits and allow the kids to pour honey on their snacks.

Story of Encouragement

Say: We can show kindness and encouragement to people in so many ways. Let's write a story where the characters **love and encourage each other.**

Directions: Staple pieces of paper together to make blank books. Give kids blank books you prepared. Have them write stories of encouragement based on what they learned in the lesson. For example: "Once there was a boy named Sam. One day Sam noticed his friend Jim was sad, so he gave him a hug. Provide crayons or colored pencils so they can illustrate their stories as well.

Chapter 50: Christ Is Coming Back

BIBLE STORY REFERENCE: Revelation 21:3–19, John 14:1–3, Colossians 3:4

MEMORY VERSE: *Look! God's dwelling place is now among the people, and he will dwell with them. They will be his people, and God himself will be with them and be their God. Revelation 21:3*

Big Idea
Heaven Is Awesome

Overview

Say: When Jesus was on Earth, he told people all about the kingdom of God. Before he left Earth and went back to heaven, he told the disciples something exciting. He told them that he was going to heaven to prepare a place for them and then he would return to get them (John 14:1–3). The same promise is true for all disciples of Jesus. If you follow Jesus, he is preparing a place for you, too (Colossians 3:4). This is very exciting news because **heaven is awesome**! It is a place where there is no sin and no sadness. It is a perfect world. We don't know when Jesus is coming back, but we do know that he has promised to return. That is very exciting news! (*Open with prayer requests, praises, and a time of prayer.*)

Bible Story

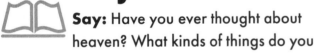

Say: Have you ever thought about heaven? What kinds of things do you hope will be there? (*Children respond.*)

Heaven is awesome! The most amazing thing about heaven is that we get to live with God. Can you imagine being able to talk with the God who made everything, including you? There will be no sadness or pain in heaven, and no one will ever die again. (*Read Revelation 21:3–4.*) **The walls of the city will be made out of gold and precious jewels** (*Read Revelations 21: 18–19.*) **It's going to be an amazing place and I'm really looking forward to living there!**

Outline
Overview
Bible Story
Opening Game
Object Lesson
Additional Optional Activities

Materials
- Bibles
- Reproducible page 249
- Cones and/or objects in room
- Thermometer
- Medicine bottle
- Adhesive bandages
- Lightbulb or flashlight
- Tissue box
- Pencils
- 1 cup baby oil
- 8 cups flour
- Mixing bowl
- Mixing spoon
- Disposable wipes
- Metallic paint
- Glitter

Opening Game: Horse Race

Materials

• Cones and/or objects in room

Tip: If possible, set up this activity in a large room—like a gym—or outside.

Preparation: Use cones or items in the room to make a path kids will follow for the race.

Say: The Bible says that when Christ comes back, he will be riding a white horse (Revelation 19:11) and all the armies of heaven will be following him on white horses as well (Revelations 19:14). In this game, you will trot like horses around the room in a race against each other.

VOLUNTEER TIDBITS

God has a reason for you to be here you never imagined. When this year is over you will look back at how much you learned about God and yourself. That there were abilities in you that you never imagined and that by being stretched beyond your comfort zone you grew that much more dependent and in love with God.

Turn to page 203 for more Volunteer Tidbits.

Object Lesson: Packing for Heaven

Materials

- Thermometer
- Medicine bottle, empty and clean
- Adhesive bandages
- Lightbulb or flashlight
- Tissue box

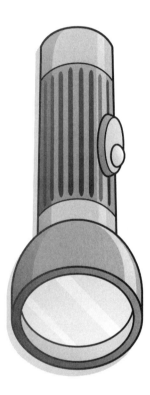

Say: Heaven is awesome. Do you remember some of the things that are so great about heaven? Let's read it again. (*Read Revelation 21:3–7, 11.*) It sounds pretty amazing. Of course, we don't take anything from Earth with us to heaven, but let's just imagine we were packing for a trip to heaven.

(*Show kids the thermometer.*) **Would we need this in heaven?** (*Children respond.*) **No, we wouldn't! There is no sickness in heaven, so we wouldn't need a thermometer.**

(*Show kids medicine and adhesive bandages.*) **What about these? Would we need medicine? Bandages?** (*Children respond.*) **Nope, we wouldn't need these either! Not only do you not get sick, but you don't get old either. You never get hurt. You won't need surgery. Everyone has a perfect body and it stays that way in heaven.**

(*Show kids lightbulb or flashlight.*) **What about this stuff?** (*Children respond.*) **You're right! We won't need it. Heaven is lit up with the glory of God. There is no night. Wow, heaven is awesome.**

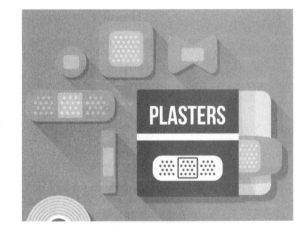

(*Show kids tissue box.*) **Of course, we won't need these either. We never cry in heaven. We are never sad or scared or lonely. We only feel happiness and peace in heaven, because we are with God. Heaven is awesome and I'm so glad God made a way for us to live with him there.**

Additional Optional Activities

Materials
- Reproducible page 249
- Pencils
- Disposable wipes

Symbols of Revelation

Say: There are so many amazing things about heaven! Let's write a letter to a friend inviting them to heaven with us.

Directions: Make a copy of the letter template for each child in the group. Have them write a letter to a friend telling them how heaven is awesome.

Materials
- 1 cup baby oil
- 8 cups flour
- Mixing bowl
- Mixing spoon
- Disposable wipes

Optional
- Food coloring

Cloud Dough

Preparation: Make cloud dough for the kids by mixing 8 cups flour with 1 cup baby oil. Optional: Add food coloring. Stir well. Make enough for each child to have some to play with.

Say: Today, I brought you some cloud dough. Of course, we know we won't be sitting on a bunch of clouds in heaven, but it's still fun to play with. And clouds can remind us that **Heaven is awesome**!

Directions: Children play with cloud dough. It can get messy, so have disposable wipes ready.

Materials
- Metallic paint
- Glitter

Dazzling View of Heaven

Say: Draw a picture of heaven based on the descriptions you've read today, remembering that **heaven is awesome**.

Directions: Children use shiny metallic paint and glitter to create a dazzling depiction of heaven. If they are stumped on what do draw, you can search for coloring pages online by typing "coloring page heaven."

Bonus Chapter: Symbols of Christmas

BIBLE STORY REFERENCE: Luke 2:1-20

MEMORY VERSE: *For to us a child is born, to us a son is given, and the government will be on his shoulders. And he will be called Wonderful Counselor, Mighty God, Everlasting Father, Prince of Peace. Isaiah 9:6*

Big Idea
Christmas Is All about Christ

Overview

Say: There are many sights and sounds at Christmas time. Sometimes, it's tough to sort out the sacred and the secular. Many of the symbols of Christmas can remind us of Christ and his birth. This year, spend some time exploring the symbols of Christmas, where they came from, and how they can help us celebrate the true reason for the season! (*Open with prayer requests, praises, and a time of prayer.*)

Introduction

Say: What are some of the things we usually see around Christmas time? (*Children respond.*)

There are lots of things to see around Christmas time. Did you know that many of our Christmas decorations have a story behind them? Today we're going to look at some of the symbols of Christmas and learn how many of them point to Christ himself, the true reason for our celebration, which is Jesus' birth. After all, **Christmas is all about Christ.**

Outline
Overview
Bible Story
Opening Game
Object Lesson
Additional Optional Activities

Materials
- **Bibles**
- **Reproducible page 250**
- **Dry-erase board**
- **Dry-erase markers**
- **Dry-erase eraser**
- **Measuring cups**
  - **Flour**
  - **Salt**
  - **Water**
  - **Bowl**
  - **Spoon**
- **Rolling pin**
- **Christmas cookie cutters**
- **Scissors**
- **Construction paper**
- **Glue**
- **Large sheet of paper**
- **Markers**
- **Notecards**
- **Tape**
- **Small candy canes**

Opening Game: Guess the Sentence

Materials

- Dry-erase board
- Dry-erase markers
- Dry-erase eraser

Directions: This game is played in a similar fashion to hang-man, but there is no hang-man involved. Think of a sentence or phrase related to Christmas (some ideas below) and write blanks on the board to match the letters in the phrase. Write the alphabet along the top of the board. Go around the room, allow each kid to guess a letter (cross out the letters in the alphabet as they guess). Fill in the blanks on the board as they guess them. For extra fun, break up the group into boys and girls teams.

Ideas to try:

- Merry Christmas!
- Do you want to build a snowman?
- It's cold outside.
- Christ is born!
- The angels told the shepherds.
- Deck the halls.

VOLUNTEER TIDBITS

It is important to remember that we are not the source of transforming lives; it is only by the hand of the Holy Spirit that it can happen. God needs people with a servant's heart, and a love for him and children to step into the space and be used.

Turn to page 207 for more Volunteer Tidbits.

Object Lesson: Symbols of Christmas

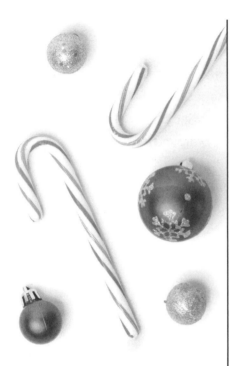

The Christmas Tree: In the early eighth century, a man named Saint Boniface, who converted the German people to Christianity, demolished the Oak of Thor, a mighty tree worshiped by the Saxons. From its roots grew a fir tree which Boniface turned into a sign of the Christian faith. People soon began putting trees in their homes in December. About the year 1500, Martin Luther brought a small tree indoors and decorated it with candles in honor of Christ's birth. Because the evergreen is green year-round, it represents hope. Its shape points upward, reminding us of God in heaven.

Gifts: Jesus himself was a gift to us at Christmas time. The wise men brought gifts to the newborn baby, which most likely inspired the idea of gift-giving at Christmas.

Candy Cane: This is one of the richest symbols of Christmas. It is shaped both like a shepherd's crook (Read Psalm 23, John 10:11) and the letter *J* for Jesus' name. The white candy symbolizes the purity of Christ and the red stripes represent the blood he shed for our sins.

Gingerbread Man: Gingerbread people remind us of God's creation of Adam in the Garden of Eden, and God's creation of each of us. A gingerbread man's body is the color of dirt, reminding us that Adam was formed from the dust. Like us, gingerbread people are not immortal. Our mortal bodies, like that of the gingerbread man's, will not live forever. Thankfully, God has given us a soul that can live forever with him in heaven.

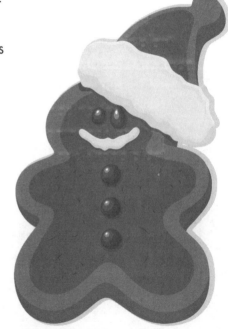

Materials

- Measuring cups
- Flour
- Salt
- Water
- Bowl
- Spoon
- Rolling pin
- Christmas cookie cutters

Tip: Borrow Christmas cookie cutters from family and friends.

Materials

- Reproducible page 250
- Scissors
- Construction paper
- Glue

Materials

- Large sheet of paper
- Markers
- Notecards
- Tape
- Small candy canes

Tip: Arrange an outing to take children to a shopping center or other place where people gather so that they can give out their Candy-Cane Messages.

Salt Dough Ornaments

Say: There are so many symbols in Christmas that show us that **Christmas is about Christ**. Let's make some ornaments together so we can give them to family and friends this Christmas.

Directions: Using the salt dough recipe on page 113, make ornaments that match the symbols of Christmas we just learned about.

Coloring and Cutting

Preparation: Copy page 250, making one for each child.

Say: Let's decorate this tree to remind us of the symbols that show us **Christmas is about Christ**.

Directions: Give a copy of page 250 to each child to cut out and glue onto a sheet of construction paper. Children color decorations and glue onto tree.

Candy-Cane Messages

Preparation: On large sheet of paper, copy the poem in the box below.

Directions: On notecards, children copy the poem from the large sheet of paper. Give each child a candy cane to tape to notecard. Tell children to hand their Candy-Cane Message to someone to share that **Christmas is about Christ**.

> Look at the Candy Cane. What do you see?
> Stripes that are red like the blood shed for me.
> White is for my Savior, who's sinless and pure!
> J is for Jesus my Lord, that's for sure!
> Spin it around, and a staff you will see.
> Jesus my Shepherd, was born for Me!

Bonus Chapter: Symbols of Easter

BIBLE STORY REFERENCE: Mark 14—16

MEMORY VERSE: *The angel said to the women, "Do not be afraid, for I know that you are looking for Jesus, who was crucified. He is not here; he has risen, just as he said. Come and see the place where he lay." Matthew 28:5–6*

Big Idea
Easter Is All about Christ

Overview

Say: There is so much to see and experience at Easter. Eggs, bunnies, chicks, and so much more! If Easter is all about the resurrection of Christ, where did all the cute animals come from? Many of the symbols of Easter, though originally pagan in nature, can help us understand the true reason for the season: Christ and his death. (*Open with prayer requests, praises, and a time of prayer.*)

Introduction

Say: What are some of the things we usually see around Easter time? (*Children respond.*)

There are lots of things to see around Easter time. Did you know that many of our Easter decorations have a story behind them? Today we're going to look at some of the symbols of Easter and learn how many of them can remind us of Christ, the true reason for our celebration.

Outline

Overview
Bible Story
Opening Game
Object Lesson
Additional Optional Activities

Materials

- **Bibles**
- **Plastic Easter eggs**
- **Colored buckets**
- **Small live animals**
- **Measuring cups**
  - **Flour**
  - **Salt**
  - **Water**
  - **Bowls**
  - **Spoons**
  - **Tin cans**
  - **Cardstock**
- **Masking tape**
- **Paintbrushes**
  - **Cardstock**
- **Watercolors**
- **Paintbrushes**
  - **Water**

Opening Game #1: Easter Egg Hunt

Materials
- Plastic Easter eggs

Preparation: Hide some eggs around the room.

Directions: Have a traditional Easter-egg hunt. If you have a wide range of ages, you can assign a certain color to each age group so that the little ones will still have a chance to find some eggs.

Materials
- Plastic Easter eggs
- Colored buckets

Opening Game #2: Easter Egg Sort

Directions: If you're looking for a little extra fun, have kids race against the clock to sort eggs by color. Give a child a bucket of colored plastic eggs. Set coordinating colored buckets in front of them (available at discount stores). The goal is to sort the eggs into the correctly colored bucket as quickly as possible. Keep track of times and have kids race against the clock and each other.

Say: The egg is a terrific symbol to point us to Christ. Though it looks still and lifeless, it is only a matter a time before a (fertilized!) egg brings forth new life.

In the same way, Christ was placed in a tomb and many people believed that was the end of the story. It looked like Christ would be lifeless forever. But Christ rose again from the dead, leaving an empty tomb behind.

Likewise, when a new chick is born, they leave behind an empty egg, reminding us of the empty tomb. Many ancient cultures, including the Persians, Greeks, and Chinese gave eggs as gifts during spring festivals.

The first recorded person to color eggs was in 1290 when Edward I of England recorded a purchase of 450 eggs to be colored or covered with gold leaf. He then gave the eggs to members of the royal household.

VOLUNTEER TIDBITS

None of you is insignificant! Remember this each week as you prepare to enter the room. "God has placed me here to be what these children need." Anticipate what God will do that day.

Object Lesson: Symbols of Easter

Materials

- Small live animals (rabbits, puppies, etc.)

Caution: Some children are allergic to animals. Check with families ahead of time or use stuffed animals.

Rabbit: In many cultures, the rabbit is a symbol of new life. Though originally tied to the celebration of spring, the bunny has also become associated with the celebration of Easter since Easter is all about new life in Christ.

Easter Lilies: The white blossoms of this flower symbolize the purity of Jesus. Lilies, which grow after the lifelessness of winter, also symbolize new life and the resurrection of Christ

Lamb: The lamb is another symbol associated with Jesus. He is referred to in the Bible as the "Lamb of God" (Revelation 5:6–14 and John 1:29). The lamb is another symbol of new life.

Pet Shop

Say: Today is an exciting day. We have some furry friends to remind us of the symbols of Easter. Let's pet them as we remember that **Easter is all about Christ**.

Directions: Borrow some small animals from friends and family. Many people have rabbits as pets and would be happy to bring them for a visit. Kids will be delighted to pet these furry friends. Be sure to have a hand washing station or hand sanitizer on hand.

Materials

- Measuring cups
- Flour
- Salt
- Water
- Bowls
- Spoons
- Tin cans

Tip: For a step by step tutorial, search online for "salt dough tomb."

Materials

- Masking tape
- Cardstock
- Watercolors
- Paintbrushes
- Water

Note: The button lamb from Chapter 38: Lost Things would also be good for this lesson.

Salt Dough Tomb

Directions: Using the salt dough recipe on page 113, prepare enough dough for each child to cover an empty tin can and make a circle of dough to cover the opening.

Say: Let's make our own empty tomb to remember the amazing fact that Jesus is risen!

Directions: Children use dough to cover an empty tin can and form a circle out of dough to represent the stone that was rolled away.

Masking Tape Cross

Say: Easter is all about Christ and how Jesus died and rose again. Let's make a craft to remind us of Jesus death and resurrection.

Directions: This is a fun way to make a beautiful art project featuring a cross. Place masking tape in the shape of a cross on some cardstock. Kids to paint entire page with watercolors. Remove tape to reveal a cross once kids are done painting.

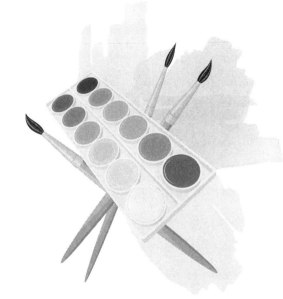

Chapter 1: Creation

Uranus

Jupiter

Earth

Saturn

Venus

Mercury

Mars

Neptune

Upset the Solar System!

Chapter 2:
Sin Enters the World

Chapter 3:
Noah's Ark

BEAR CAMEL LION TURTLE

GAZELLE KANGAROO ELEPHANT RHINOCEROS

PIG KOALA PORCUPINE MONKEY

COW BEAVER OSTRICH MEERKAT

Chapter 3:
Noah's Ark

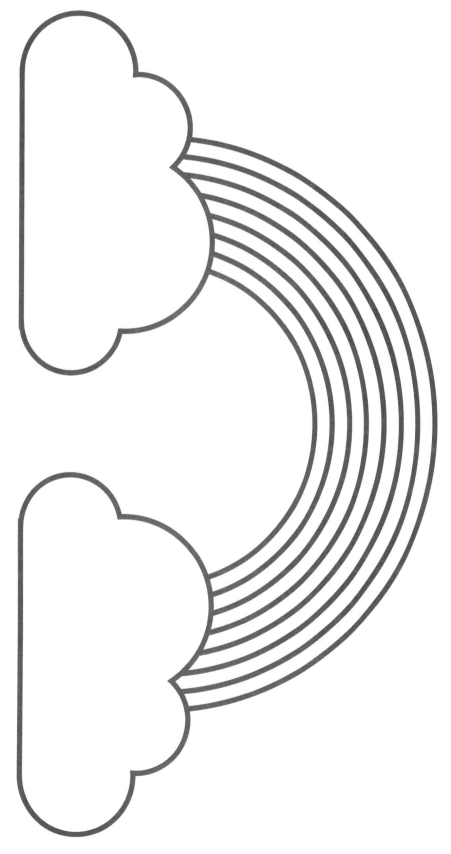

Chapter 5:
Abraham and God's Promise

Chapter 6:
Isaac and His Sons

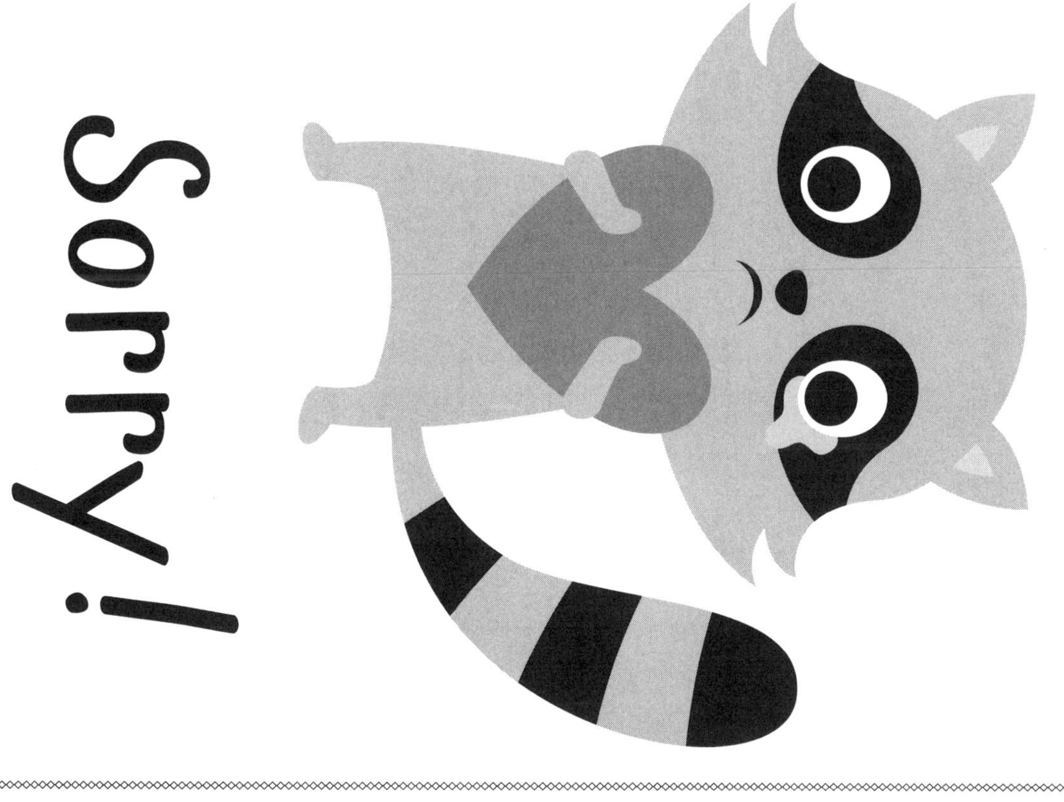

Chapter 7:
Jacob's Twelve Sons

Chapter 7:
Jacob's Twelve Sons

Chapter 8:
Joseph in Egypt

A 𓅬 , 𓂝   **I** 𓏭   **Q** 𓈎   **Y** 𓏭𓏭

B 𓃀   **J** 𓆓   **R** 𓂋   **Z** 𓊃

C 𓎡 , 𓇌   **K** 𓎡   **S** 𓋴

D 𓂧   **L** 𓃭   **T** 𓏏

E 𓇌   **M** 𓅓   **U** 𓅱

F 𓆑   **N** 𓈖 , 𓈗   **V** 𓆑

G 𓎼 , 𓏭𓏭   **O** 𓍯   **W** 𓅱 , 𓏲

H 𓉔   **P** 𓊪   **X** 𓋴𓊃

~~~~~~

ANNA 𓅬𓈖𓈗𓅬   DIANA 𓂧𓇌𓅬𓈖𓅬   ROBERT 𓂋𓍯𓃀𓇌𓂋𓏏

ADAM 𓅬𓂧𓅬𓅬   PETER 𓊪𓇌𓏏𓇌𓂋   MARIA 𓅓𓅬𓂋𓇌𓅬

Chapter 9:
Baby Moses Is Saved

Chapter 10:
Moses and Pharaoh

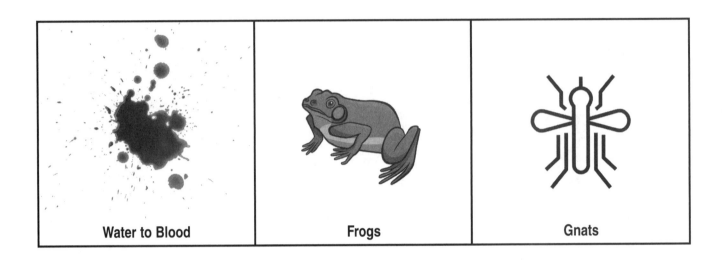

Water to Blood

Frogs

Gnats

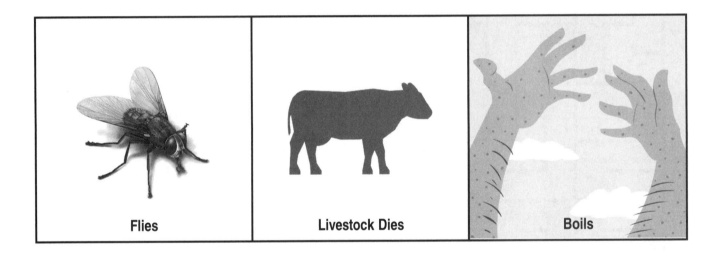

Flies

Livestock Dies

Boils

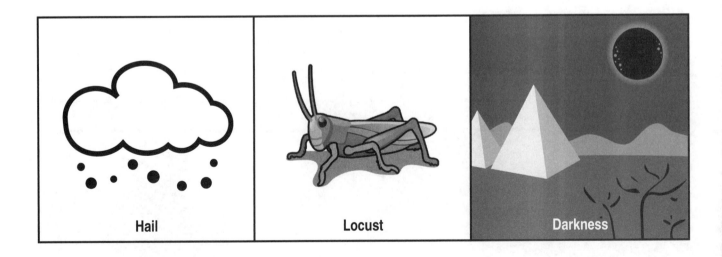

Hail

Locust

Darkness

Chapter II:
Israelites in the Desert

Chapter 13:
Ehud

Chapter 15:
Samuel

Riding a Bike	**Playing Basketball**	**Washing a Car**	**Driving a Car**
Taking a Nap	**Burying a Treasure**	**Climbing a Tree**	**Going Down a Slide**
Building a Sand Castle	**Building a Campfire**	**Baking a Cake**	**Feeding the Birds**
Going Bowling	**Milking a Cow**	**Paddling a Canoe**	**Sewing on a Button**

Chapter 16:
David as Shepherd

The Lord is _____.

He takes care of _____.

_____.

He gives me _____.

_____.

He protects me so I don't need to be afraid of

_____.

I will always _____.

_____.

Chapter 18: King Solomon

Chapter 20:
Christ Is Coming Back

Chapter 20:
Elijah

Chapter 22: Jonah

Chapter 24:
Daniel

Chapter 25:
Summary of the Story of Esther

Long ago, in Persia, there was a king named Xerses and a queen named Vashti. The king grew angry at the queen for not attending one of his banquets. He banished Vashti and chose to replace her with a new queen.

A search was made throughout the whole kingdom. Soon, a Jewish girl named Esther became the new queen. Mordecai, Esther's uncle, encouraged Esther to hide her Jewish faith from the king, and she did.

The king had an advisor named **Haman** who had become a very powerful man. When the king made **Haman** the new Prime Minister, all the people in the land were to bow down to him.

But Mordecai refused to bow down to **Haman**. This made **Haman** furious. **Haman** asked the king to authorize a royal decree that would destroy all the Jews. Surprisingly, the king agreed.

Mordecai heard about the awful decree and sent Esther a message. He told her what **Haman** was planning on doing and asked her to speak to the king.

Esther was afraid. She was not allowed to visit the king without being invited. If she did, the king could have her killed. Even though it meant she might die, Esther chose to try and save her people from **Haman**'s evil plan. She fasted and prayed for three days. Mordecai and the other Jewish people did the same.

When Esther went to see the king, he was gracious to her. She invited the king and **Haman** to a banquet, but she did not talk about **Haman**'s plan at this banquet. Instead, she invited King Xerses and **Haman** to a second banquet on the following night.

On the night of the first banquet, the king could not sleep so he ordered the books of history to be read to him. He heard about the time Mordecai had saved his life from an assassination attempt, but Mordecai had not been properly honored.

The next day the king asked **Haman**, for ideas to honor someone. **Haman** thought the king was trying to honor him, so **Haman** told the king to host a parade and let the man ride on a royal horse, wearing a royal robe.

The king liked **Haman**'s ideas and told him to do all those things for Mordecai. **Haman** was shocked and furious, but he obeyed the king.

Later that night, **Haman** and the king attended Esther's second banquet. It was at this banquet that Esther begged the king for the life of her people. She revealed that she was Jewish and that **Haman** had plotted to destroy all the Jewish people.

The king promised to help save Esther and her people. He was so angry at **Haman** that he had him killed.

Esther's courage saved her people and through her story, we can see that **God always has a plan.**

Chapter 25:
Esther

Start

Finish

Chapter 27:
Time of Waiting

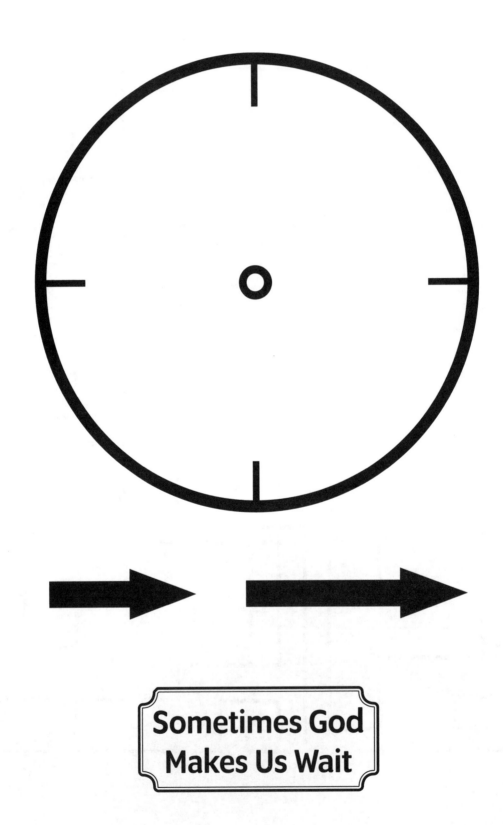

Sometimes God
Makes Us Wait

Chapter 28:
Jesus Is Born

Chapter 29:
Wise Men Visit Jesus

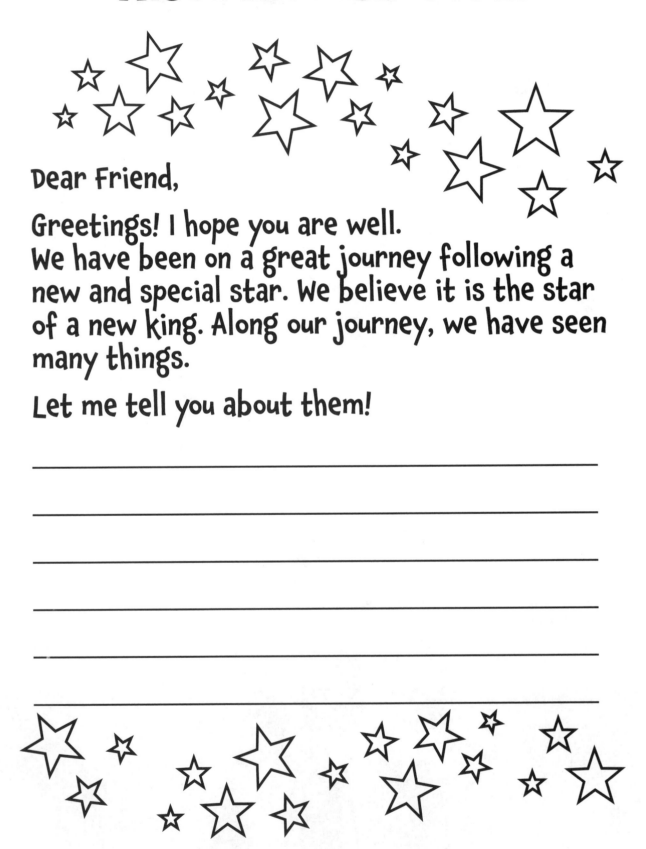

Dear Friend,

Greetings! I hope you are well.
We have been on a great journey following a new and special star. We believe it is the star of a new king. Along our journey, we have seen many things.

Let me tell you about them!

_____

_____

_____

_____

_____

Chapter 30:
John the Baptist

Chapter 30:
John the Baptist

Chapter 33:
Jesus Feeds 5,000 People

Materials: • This page and page 238 • dessert-sized paper plates • curling ribbon • hole punch • glue

Preparation: Copy both reproducible pages, making one of each for each child.

Directions: 1. Children cut out and color the patterns. 2. Children glue the bread and the woven piece to the plate to form a basket. 3. Children punch two holes around the bottom of each plate and at the mouth of each fish. 4. Children cut lengths of curling ribbon and tie the fish to the bottoms of their plates. Use scissors to curl the ends of the ribbons. 5. Encourage the children to hang their verse baskets where they can be seen at home.

Chapter 33:
Jesus Feeds 5,000 People

 Top 50 Instant Bible Lessons® for Elementary

Chapter 34:
Jesus Calms the Storm

Chapter 35: Mary and Martha

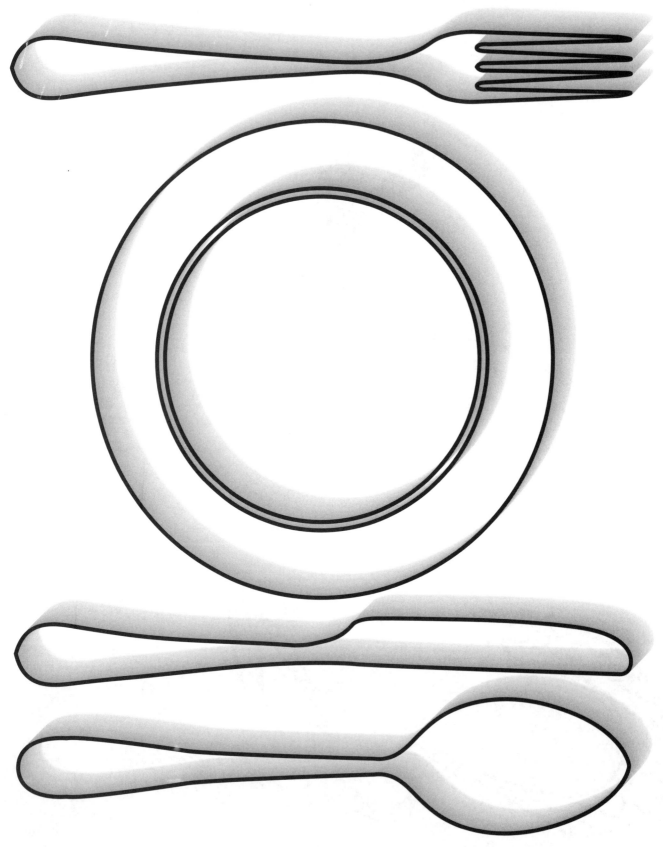

Chapter 37:
The Good Samaritan

Chapter 38:
Lost Things

! Help the shepherd find the lost sheep

1

2

3

Luke 15:4-6

Chapter 40: Workers in the Vineyard

"So the last will be first, and the first will be last."

Matthew 20:16

Big Idea:
God gives us mercy.

Materials: • cardstock • brads

Preparation: Copy this page onto cardstock, making one for each child.

Directions: Children cut out arrows and clock face. Then they push one brad through both arrows and the center of the clock and secure.

Say: God wants everyone to feel important and loved. He shows each of us mercy no matter when we learn about him. He wants us all to be in a relationship with him.

Chapter 43:
Jesus Gives Final Instructions
I am a Disciple of Christ

	Read my Bible	Prayer	Show kindness
Monday	☐	☐	☐
Tuesday	☐	☐	☐
Wednesday	☐	☐	☐
Thursday	☐	☐	☐
Friday	☐	☐	☐
Saturday	☐	☐	☐
Sunday	☐	☐	☐

Say: Each day, grow closer to God by reading your Bible, praying and showing kindness to others. Before bed each night, check off if you were able to do this. How did it make your day better?

Chapter 44:
The Holy Spirit Comes

Black headband, cut two from black construction paper.

Chapter 46:
Set Free from Sin

Name: _____

Set Free from Sin

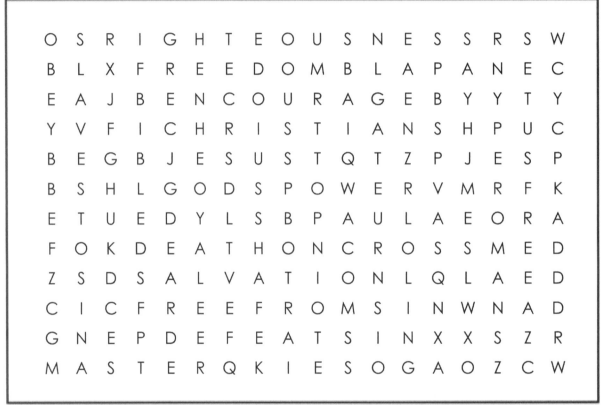

```
O S R I G H T E O U S N E S S R S W
B L X F R E E D O M B L A P A N E C
E A J B E N C O U R A G E B Y Y T Y
Y V F I C H R I S T I A N S H P U C
B E G B J E S U S T Q T Z P J E S P
B S H L G O D S P O W E R V M R F K
E T U E D Y L S B P A U L A E O R A
F O K D E A T H O N C R O S S M E D
Z S D S A L V A T I O N L Q L A E D
C I C F R E E F R O M S I N W N A D
G N E P D E F E A T S I N X X S Z R
M A S T E R Q K I E S O G A O Z C W
```

Find the following words in the puzzle.
Words are hidden ➡ and ⬇.

BIBLE	**FREEDOM**	**RIGHTEOUSNESS**
CHRISTIANS	**GOD'S POWER**	**ROMANS**
DEATH ON A CROSS	**JESUS**	**SALVATION**
DEFEAT SIN	**MASTER**	**SET US FREE**
ENCOURAGE	**OBEY**	**SLAVES TO SIN**
FREE FROM SIN	**PAUL**	

Chapter 47:
The Body of Christ

Materials: • cardstock

Preparation: Copy this page onto cardstock, making two copies. Cut out each picture. Set cards facedown on a table in a grid pattern.

Directions: Children take turns turning over two cards to try see if they match. If the cards match, the child takes the cards. If they don't match, child turns cards facedown again.

Say: Each of us is different. God made us different to help others and do different jobs at our church.
What are some things that you are good at that? How can you use that to help others?

Chapter 48:
Armor of God

HELMET OF **SALVATION**

THE **WHOLE** **ARMOR OF GOD**

EPHESIANS 6:10-20

SWORD OF THE WORD

SHIELD OF **FAITH**

BELT OF **TRUTH**

BREASTPLATE OF **RIGHTEOUSNESS**

SHOES OF **GOODNEWS**

Chapter 50:
Christ Is Coming Back

Dear _____ ,

Did you know that heaven is awesome?
Some of the amazing things about heaven are:

_____

_____

Anyone can go to heaven when they
trust God to forgive their sins. I hope
that you will come to heaven, too!

Love, _____ .

Bonus Chapter: Christmas

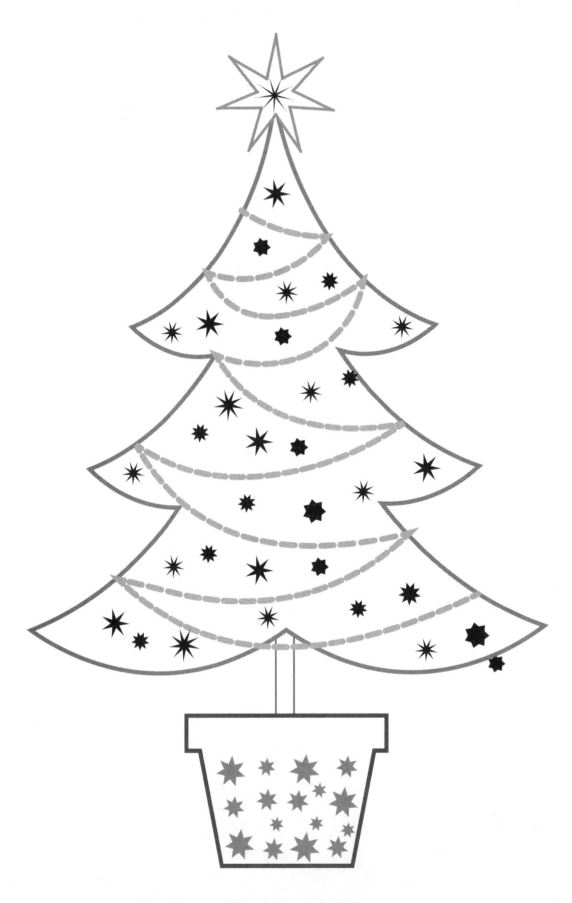

R⊘SEKiDZ® RESOURCES FOR TEACHERS

Look for more great titles in our popular Top 50 series!

Here are some favorites:

Top 50 Instant Bible Lessons for Preschool

AGES 2–5, 208 PAGES, PAPERBACK

Teach the Top 50 lessons from the popular Instant Bible Lessons series. The *Top 50 Instant Bible Lessons for Preschoolers* includes quick and easy-to-use resources for Sunday school teachers with reproducible hand-outs, arts and crafts templates, puzzles, games, and step-by-step instructions.

Product Code: R50002
ISBN: 978-1-62862-497-7

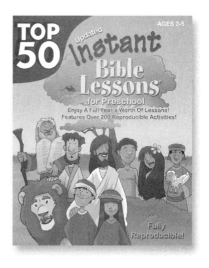

Top 50 Object Lessons: Games & Activities

AGES 5–10, 208 PAGES, PAPERBACK

The easy-to-follow, volunteer-friendly book *Top 50 Bible Object Lessons* creates opportunities for children to remember the main theme using science and everyday objects. Teach kids key Bible stories plus twenty bonus holiday and favorite game object lessons. Quick and easy-to-use for Sunday School, midweek programs, homeschool, and more! Includes reproducible pages.

Product Code: R50009
ISBN: 978-1-62862-504-2

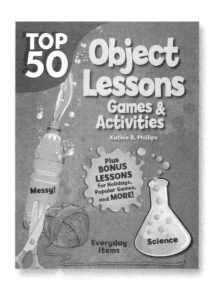

Top 50 Memory Verse Lessons: with Games & Activities

AGES 5–10, 208 PAGES, PAPERBACK

Memory verses are vital to hiding God's Word in the heart and mind of every child. *Top 50 Memory Verses with Games & Activities* makes verse memorization easy! Kids will have so much fun, they won't realize they're memorizing Scripture. The book is packed with fun, interactive, creative, and engaging ways to get children excited about Scripture.

Product Code: R50010
ISBN: 978-1-62862-505-9

Big Puzzles for Little Hands: The Bible Tells Me So

AGES 3–8, 96 PAGES, PAPERBACK

Young children are very inquisitive and love to learn new things—the most important of which are Bible truths. With *Big Puzzles for Little Hands,* you can provide that scriptural instruction using fun, age-based activities that kids love. From mazes to color-by-number to seek-and-find, these puzzles will help even the smallest students learn more about God's love and his plan for their lives. Over 80 lessons from the Old and New Testaments! Every lesson includes: Memory verse; Bible story reference; tips for teacher talk; easy instruction; reproducible pages.

Product Code: R36834
ISBN: 978-1-88535-880-6

The Super-Sized Book of Bible Puzzles

AGES 5–10, 256 PAGES, PAPERBACK

Fun Bible learning with pencils and crayons! *The Super-Sized Book of Bible Puzzles* has over 210 fun searches, mazes, pictures, and puzzles that help kids learn their favorite Bible stories from the Old and New Testaments. It is perfect for families, Sunday school teachers, home schools, and Christian school leaders. Answers included.

Product Code: R38251
ISBN: 978-1-58411-142-9

The Super-Sized Book of Bible Crafts

AGES 5–10, 256 PAGES, PAPERBACK

The Super-Sized Book of Bible Crafts is perfect for use at home, in church, or in Sunday School. Designed for children ages 5 to 10 years, this reproducible book is jam-packed with fun crafts and exciting projects that help children to better understand God's Word. Each project includes clear directions on how to build each craft using simple, everyday household items and materials. Includes a craft index by theme in the back.

Product Code: R38252
ISBN: 978-1-58411-150-4